Routledge Revivals

An Introduction to the Study of Education

First Published in 1971, *An Introduction to the Study of Education* is a basic introduction to the curriculum of education which will be of interest to students in colleges of education as well as to sixth formers. The six contributors, all well known in the educational field, consider different aspects of the study of education. J.W. Tibble himself considers the development of the study of education. D.J. Watts contributes a chapter on educational psychology. Anne Dufton looks at the sociology of education, while its history is examined by Malcolm Seaborne and its philosophy by R.F. Dearden. The relationship between theory and practice is considered by Harold Entwistle, and a final chapter, by J.W. Tibble, looks at the curriculum courses available in Britain.

An Introduction to the Study of Education

An Outline for the Student

Edited by J. W. Tibble

First published in 1971
by Routledge & Kegan Paul.

This edition first published in 2024 by Routledge
4 Park Square, Milton Park, Abingdon, Oxon, OX14 4RN

and by Routledge
605 Third Avenue, New York, NY 10017

Routledge is an imprint of the Taylor & Francis Group, an informa business

© 1971 Routledge & Kegan Paul Ltd.

All rights reserved. No part of this book may be reprinted or reproduced or utilised in any form or by any electronic, mechanical, or other means, now known or hereafter invented, including photocopying and recording, or in any information storage or retrieval system, without permission in writing from the publishers.

Publisher's Note
The publisher has gone to great lengths to ensure the quality of this reprint but points out that some imperfections in the original copies may be apparent.

Disclaimer
The publisher has made every effort to trace copyright holders and welcomes correspondence from those they have been unable to contact.

A Library of Congress record exists under LCCN:

ISBN: 978-1-032-79281-1 (hbk)
ISBN: 978-1-003-49138-5 (ebk)
ISBN: 978-1-032-79283-5 (pbk)

Book DOI 10.4324/9781003491385

Edited by J. W. Tibble
Emeritus Professor of Education
University of Leicester

An introduction to
THE STUDY OF EDUCATION

An outline for the student

Routledge & Kegan Paul London

First published 1971
by Routledge & Kegan Paul Ltd
Broadway House, 68–74 Carter Lane
London EC4V 5EL
Reprinted 1975
Printed in Great Britain by
Redwood Burn Limited
Trowbridge & Esher

© Routledge & Kegan Paul Ltd 1971

No part of this book may be reproduced in
any form without permission from the
publisher, except for the quotation of brief
passages in criticism

ISBN 0 7100 7080 2 (c)
ISBN 0 7100 7081 0 (p)

Contents

	Introduction	1
1	**The Development of the Study of Education**	5
	J. W. Tibble *Emeritus Professor of Education* *University of Leicester*	
2	**Educational Psychology**	18
	D. G. Watts *Senior Counsellor* *The Open University*	
3	**The Sociology of Education**	44
	Anne Dufton *Dean of the Faculty of Social Sciences* *Ulster College, Belfast*	
4	**The History of Education**	65
	Malcolm Seaborne *Senior Lecturer in Education* *University of Leicester*	

5 The Philosophy of Education 80
R. F. Dearden
*Lecturer in the Philosophy of Education
University of London Institute of Education*

6 The Relationship between Theory and Practice 95
Harold Entwistle
*Associate Professor, Department of Education
Sir George Williams University, Montreal*

7 Curriculum Courses 114
J. W. Tibble

Index 119

Introduction

This book has been planned and written for intending teachers, whether they be students in sixth forms of secondary schools or older people seeking entry to a college of education, university undergraduates contemplating a fourth year of professional training or students who have just embarked on a course in a college or department of education. For all these there is a common problem: the study of education, which will be an important part of the course, is not a subject they are likely to have met in their previous experience. For college of education students there will be other subjects in the course, main or special subjects studied for three years and shorter courses in curriculum or professional subjects chosen from the range of the school curriculum: they have met all these at earlier stages of their schooling and will have a fairly good idea of what is involved in their study of them in college. Education, in the sense used in this book, they have not met in this way, and in most instances they will have only a vague idea of what it involves. The university undergraduates contemplating a one-year graduate certificate course in a university department or college of education are in a similar situation. In their case about half the course will be concerned with the study of education and the other half directly or indirectly with its practice. We think that many of them will be interested to find out in advance about the nature of this new subject and that such knowledge may help to make their study more effective in the early stages of the course.

This leads me to refer to a second reason for the writing of this

2 Introduction

book. It is not just that the students in question have not experienced the study of education before; it is also that what they have experienced in their schooling and the way they conceive their future roles as teachers may well give rise to misconceptions about the nature and function of the subject, and in particular about the relationship between the theory and practice of education. Students seldom doubt the value of the 'school practice' ingredient in their courses; they are often critical of the 'theory' because it does not 'tell them the answer' to the sort of questions which rise to the young teacher's lips: e.g. how to control a class, how to teach reading, how to question effectively, how to test the success of a lesson, etc. This is to misconceive the nature and purpose of educational theory, and the student's earlier (and possibly his present) experience is likely to reinforce this misconception. As an American observer has pointed out:

> In our educational system, the essential psychological similarity between each succeeding level of schooling remains unchanged. From elementary through graduate school, there is a teacher in a room with a group of students. The teacher rewards, or reinforces, the answers he wishes to follow the questions he poses. However, open issues by definition have no particular 'right' answers; a problem solving, not a rote memorization-and-recall approach, is required in learning to understand issues.*

He goes on to advocate a preliminary seminar in colleges of education in which students learn how to explore with members of staff the kind of open-ended issues that the study of education largely involves. The point I am making, which is more fully discussed by Dr Entwistle in chapter 6 of this book, is that one cannot just take the relating of theory and practice for granted; students need educating in how to relate them, and this would include an understanding of the nature of both.

There is a third reason for the writing of this book, and that is the relatively rapid changes which have taken place in recent years in the study of education itself. This means that the impressions of it which the student gets from older teachers will reflect the past rather than the present state of study in the colleges and departments.

*Herbert Garber, 'The College Teacher and His Class: A Modern Anachronism?', *The Journal of Teacher Education*, Vol. xviii, No. 3 (Fall 1967).

In the first chapter I describe the changes that have taken place and the nature of the subject as it has come to be accepted in most colleges and departments today. This is followed by chapters on each of the contributory disciplines and one on the relationship between theory and practice. The final chapter deals with curriculum courses which have a bridging function, in that they are intended to relate the study of the various subjects of the school curriculum with the central study of education.

J. W. T.

1

The Development of the Study of Education

J. W. Tibble

Compared with subjects like mathematics, history and languages, the study of education is of very recent origin. Indeed, it is only within the last decade that the fully developed form of the subject as described in this book has come to be accepted and taught in colleges and departments of education. The subject developed piecemeal during the present century, and it is the purpose of this chapter to outline this development before considering the characteristic features of the subject as we see it today.

The training of teachers came into being in this country in the 1840s with the establishment of a system of bounties in aid of the salaries of pupil teachers, Queen's Scholarships towards maintenance in training colleges and certificate examinations for adult teachers who had gone through one or another process of professional preparation. The pupil teacher system was essentially an apprenticeship entered into at the age of fourteen by brighter elementary school pupils. Attached to an experienced teacher, they stayed on at school continuing their study of the subjects in the elementary curriculum and at the same time gradually learning, by imitation and participation, the skills involved in class control and organization. The 1872 syllabus for the certificate examination shows the essentially practical nature of the training in what later became the education section of the course. It prescribed questions on the best methods of teaching the three Rs and other subjects of elementary instruction for the first-year students. The second-year syllabus prescribed (1) teaching a class in the presence of

H.M.I., (2) answering questions in writing on the following subjects: (a) the different methods of organizing an elementary school, (b) the form of school registers, the mode of keeping them and making returns from them, (c) the mode of teaching geography, history and grammar and (3) questions of moral discipline.

The early training colleges embodied a similar emphasis on practical training, following the lead of Dr Andrew Bell, pioneer of teacher training at the Glasgow Seminary: 'It is by attending the schools, seeing what is going on there, and taking a share in the office of tuition, that teachers are to be formed, and not by lectures and abstract instructions.'*[1]

C. H. Judd, in his comparative study of teacher training early in the twentieth century, has this to say:

> The evolution of the pupil teacher plan explains many of the characteristics of the training colleges. Especially is this true with respect to the great emphasis which is laid in all training colleges upon practice teaching. The apprenticeship idea has been carried over and influences the actual organization of the teaching force and the program of teachers' colleges in a most emphatic degree.

He goes on to note:

> In striking contrast with this emphasis on practical education is the relative neglect of education theory. One is very much impressed by the fact that in the English training colleges the whole theoretical side of pedagogy has a very meager and abstract treatment.[2]

An observer writing ten years after Judd noted a change that had taken place in recent years towards a more scientific kind of training, based on the study of psychology, though he goes on to point out some conditions for the successful operation of such courses. These include 'lecturers of high qualifications and long and varied experience, as well as students with mature and trained minds and leisure for sustained thought'.[3]

The beginnings of the application of psychology to courses of education can, in fact, be found in the last decade of the nineteenth century. The 1895 syllabus for the certificate examination showed little change from the 1872 syllabus, already referred to, in the

*It would seem that the majority of those who have completed a course of training and have been asked to evaluate it, agree with Dr Bell.

first two years of the course. But for those who stayed on for a third year, the syllabus was headed 'The Art, Theory and History of Teaching', and it prescribed the study of the following: the life and work of Dr Arnold, R. H. Quick's *Essays on Educational Reformers*, Dr Bain's *Education as a Science* and Sully's *The Teacher's Handbook of Psychology*.

These references indicate the introduction into training courses of two of the main strands making up the study of education, as described in this book – educational psychology and the history of education – but, of course, not in the more developed form that these subjects have today. Dr A. Bain was a pioneer in promoting the transition from the traditional 'mental philosophy' to the new 'scientific psychology' and in the relating of this to education. He foreshadowed many ideas which were more fully developed later and was critical of those twin concepts, 'faculty psychology' and 'formal training', which dominated educational theory and practice throughout the nineteenth century. A textbook of 1884 gives the prevailing doctrine in this form: 'The objects of education are: to strengthen the faculties that are too weak, to restrain those that are too vigorous, to store the intellect with moral, religious, scientific, and general knowledge and to direct all to their proper objects.'[4]

James Sully, as the different editions of his *Teacher's Handbook of Psychology* clearly show, was also a pioneer in the replacement of 'faculty psychology' by 'developmental psychology'. He was indeed the first to introduce systematic instruction on child psychology into courses for teachers, and he encouraged his students to undertake studies of individual children. The first edition of his *Teacher's Handbook*, published in 1886, dealt with mental development mainly in terms of the growth of the 'faculties' of the mind. 'One of the most valuable doctrines of modern psychology is that there is a uniform order of development of the faculties', and he referred to memory training, for example, as designed to produce 'a good type of the acquisitive or learning faculty in general'. But by the time of his fifth edition in 1909 he is writing as follows: 'In these days there is no excuse for forgetting that the child is a living organism which grows by the exercise of its own functional activity; and that the work of the educator is to excite and to direct this activity in a way most favourable to sound a complete development of mind.' His statement about memory training in this edition is much more cautious, and new

8 J. W. Tibble

material dealing with recent work in child study, social psychology, emotions and sentiments and the development of individuality indicate the new trends affecting 'educational psychology'.

The years just before and after the turn of the century were indeed seminal ones both for the development of modern psychology as a subject and for its application to the process of education. The first decade of the century saw the founding of most of the major schools of modern psychology – psychoanalysis, hormic psychology, behaviourism, Gestalt psychology – but a considerable time lag ensued before these new lines of investigation began to have an impact on courses of study in colleges and departments of education. In the period 1890 to 1910, as W. S. Monroe pointed out, 'the psychological background relating to learning consisted of a mixture of modified faculty psychology, Herbartian apperception, associationism (structural and functional) and physiological psychology.'[5] By the 1920s, however, important changes were discernible both in the organization of the professional side of the courses and in the content of the courses. Traditionally this work had been organized by a Master or Mistress of Method who usually had charge of a practice or demonstration school attached to the college. He was the college equivalent of the Master in the pupil teacher system to whom the student was attached as an apprentice. The Master of Method gave demonstration lessons in the school, and the students gave criticism lessons in his presence. The 'Method' here being demonstrated and practised was at bottom a variant of what was called in the mid-nineteenth century when it emerged 'the Simultaneous Method', to distinguish it from the Monitorial system in which monitors tutored small groups of children under the supervision of a master. In the Simultaneous Method the Master taught a whole class of children, maybe sixty or more, at the same time, and the Method denoted the skills of class control, exposition, questioning, etc. that were involved in this. Most readers of this will have participated in 'lessons' which embodied this method, for it is still commonly used, especially in secondary schools. However by the 1920s other ways of organizing learning were becoming accepted and applied mainly in the infant and junior ranges, but to some extent also in secondary schools.

These 'new' methods had their origins in the writings of J. J. Rousseau and the educational work of Basedow, Pestalozzi,

Fellenberg and Froebel. They shifted the focus of attention from the teacher as the dispenser of knowledge and manipulator of groups of children to the teacher as provider of learning situations which meet the needs of children in small groups or working as individuals. What was needed by the teacher in this situation was certainly not 'the' method or even 'a' method so much as experience and understanding of children and their individual differences, the characteristics of their learning at different stages of their development, dexterity and flexibility in devising the appropriate materials and techniques to match a child's needs.

In this changing educational climate, the term Master or Mistress of Method became obsolete and was replaced by Lecturer in Education. The process was accelerated by the founding of new and larger training colleges by the local education authorities after the 1902 Education Act to supplement the traditional voluntary colleges. The number of students to be catered for on school practice meant that many schools in the area had to be used, and the use of a special demonstration or practising school gradually declined. Instead the Lecturer in Education and also lecturers in other subjects visited the students several times a week in their schools and gave advice and criticism in a more informal way. The Lecturer in Education, from the 1920s on, also found a growing body of knowledge available to him. The most influential book at this level in the period between the two world wars was Sir Percy Nunn's *Education: Its Data and First Principles*, which was published in 1920; a new impression was issued almost yearly up to 1930 when a revised edition appeared; a third edition, revised with a new chapter on Mental Measurement, was issued in 1945. The 'data' of Nunn's book were drawn mainly from the fields of biology and psychology, especially the 'hormic' psychology developed by William McDougall in his popular *Introduction to Social Psychology* (1908). The most fundamental of the 'principles' which Nunn professed to derive from his data was the reaffirmation of 'the infinite value of the individual person' and 'his ultimate responsibility for his own destiny'. The importance of Nunn's book is that it set the seal of academic respectability on the ideas underlying the progressive education movement. The notion that the roots of human behaviour were to be found in instinctive tendencies, the view of the child's growth as a process of the unfolding of these tendencies and their combination in 'sentiments', the definition of the aims of education in terms of the development of individuality – these became approved doctrines of the 'principles of education' courses in colleges and departments of education. The changed context of educational psychology in training courses was described by Professor Hamley in 1936, and its influence on practice is described by Professor H. S. N. McFarland in these terms:

> From it stem all the classroom methods, all the apparatus and text books associated with child centred education. . . . Some of the pedagogic practices stemming from child study are: the more careful guiding of education materials to match differing degrees of ability; the emphasis on activities, concrete objects and pictures as valuable precursors or companions of the spoken and written word; and the greater attention paid to physical, emotional and social education as being the complements of intellectual education.[6]

Thus the main strand in the study of education down to the Second World War was provided by educational psychology, and the core of this was the study of children through a series of developmental stages from birth to maturity. Societies for the promotion of child study date from the 1890s; a journal, the *Paidologist*, was founded in 1899 and renamed *Child Study* in 1908. James Sully, Cyril Burt, W. H. Winch and W. Boyd were pioneers in this field, and between the world wars departments devoted to the systematic psychological study of children were instituted. Susan Isaac's work at the London Institute of Education and C. W. Valentine's at Birmingham University provided plentiful source material. Jean Piaget's early contributions to this tradition appeared in English translations from 1926 on, and his later contributions on the stages of concept formation by children have become required reading (or at any rate reading about) in all education courses.

Another major preoccupation for educational psychology in its development after the First World War was the testing and assessment of human abilities, in particular of general intelligence. The contributions of Cyril Burt, appointed by the L.C.C. in 1913 as the first educational psychologist, of Charles Spearman at University College and Godfrey Thomson at Moray House, Edinburgh, answered the need for more effective selection procedures in the developing secondary system. For a generation, the determination of I.Q.s not only became a minor industry, but it also had some characteristics of a religious cult; the belief in a fixed, biologically determined I.Q. was used to justify the segregation of children in different types of school and in different streams within schools.

The report of a survey of the place of educational psychology in training college courses for the year 1959 estimated that 40 per cent of the time devoted to the study of education was spent on this aspect of it and that of this 40 per cent, a quarter was concerned with child development, a quarter with learning and adjustment and a third with attainments, abilities and non-statistical aspects of psychometrics. The report also comments:

> On the whole the approach appeared to be empirical rather than theoretical. The questions on learning, for example, seemed to be based on a knowledge of established classroom practice together with some of the more important experimental findings. Very few asked for general underlying theoretical principles about learning. Similarly with child psychology and developmental psychology, there were few questions on general principles, most of the questions being essentially descriptive.[7]

The report also noted that some important topics appeared rarely in the examination papers; among these were questions on Piaget's work, on transfer of training, on aspects of thinking and problem solving and on group relations and social factors in classroom motivation and reinforcement.

With regard to the last of these (and the first too), one assumes a time lag between a change in the emphasis or content of a course and the appearance of that change in the examination papers. Dr C. M. Fleming, writing in 1952, had noted a change of emphasis in the core courses on child development:

> Attention turned from social setting to social relationship, from membership of society to membership of group ... to an awareness of the potency of social pressures ... and an awareness of conflicting tensions in social situations. ... The study of child personality was recognized as a study not of the child as he is, but as the study of the child in relation to his teachers, to his parents, to his contemporaries.[8]

Support for this change of emphasis came from the development of new ideas and techniques in the field of social psychology, in particular the work of J. L. Moreno, founder and developer of Sociometrics.

Parallel with this change of emphasis within educational psychology, there occurred, in the late 1950s, pioneer contributions from the field of another basic discipline, sociology, now recognized by most universities as a 'proper' subject for study and research. As we have seen, the main emphasis in the inter-war years was on the definition and measurement of differences among children, on the assumption that the most important of these were biologically determined. By testing, the level and type of a child's educational capacities could be determined, and he could be sent to the kind of secondary school which enabled him best to realize these capacities. It now became clear, as evidence in sociological surveys by Floud and Halsey, Jackson and Marsden[9] emphasized, that social factors such as the nature of the home background and neighbourhood, the wealth and occupational level of parents, the qualities of primary schools have a significant influence in determining to what extent an individual can gain access to and utilize the educational facilities provided. Selective procedures, however carefully designed, could not eliminate those factors.

Whilst studies of educational opportunities have continued and have greatly influenced the reports of official committees,[10] the scope of work in the sociology of education widened considerably in the 1960s and new lines of enquiry have been opened up. These include studies of the place of different types of schools in the educational system, the relation of schools to the communities they serve, social determinants of educability, e.g. language, and the application of organization theory to understanding the internal dynamics of a school.[11]

For the third and fourth main strands in the study of education as we now see it, we turn back to the reference in the 1895 syllabus for third-year students to the life and work of Arnold of Rugby and Quick's *Educational Reformers*. Quick's *Educational Reformers* appeared in 1868 but made little impact in this country until 1890, when a second edition was printed.[12] The educational climate was now more propitious for the development of studies in the history of education, and between 1897 and 1920 the Cambridge University Press published a remarkable series of contributions.[13] The Cambridge Syndicate, to provide for the training of secondary teachers, had been set up in 1879, and the history of education had a prominent place in the courses of lectures provided. A minority report of the Cross Commission had advocated not only the training of teachers in universities but also the formation of education faculties to foster the academic study of education and research in this subject. From 1890 on, 'university day training colleges' were set up in many universities and university colleges. These provided, at first, a three-year course with work for a degree and for professional training done concurrently; after 1909 these were changed to four-year consecutive courses with work for the degree taken in the first three years and the professional training mainly in the fourth year. This is still the pattern in the university departments of education which developed out of the day training colleges. The university setting and the longer course provided more scope for the development of the study of education, and particularly of the history of education, for history was a long established study and graduates in this subject had received the basic training necessary for applying it in the field of educational history. A pioneer of this development was J. W. Adamson, appointed head of the training department at King's College, London, in 1890. His *Pioneers of Modern Education, 1600–1700* was published in 1905 and his *Short History of Education* in 1919. Foster Watson, who became Professor of Education at Aberystwyth in 1894, was another of the pioneers with his study of Vives and his books on the English grammar schools. *The Syllabus of a course on the History of Education in England, 1800–1911*, published by Michael Sadler in 1911, was one of the earliest attempts to work out a detailed course with book lists for each lecture. Other contributors to the development of this subject were F. A. Cavanagh, W. H. Woodward, R. L. Archer and Frank Smith.

The history of education, in the courses provided by the university departments, normally included both a study of English educational institutions and of the work of great educators, from Plato to John Dewey. The departments also actively promoted research and higher degree studies in this field.[14] In the colleges, after the setting up of regional examining boards in the 1920s, references to historical studies, both of the great educators and of the English educational system, began to appear in the syllabuses. While the college courses were of two years' duration and with the main emphasis on educational psychology, it is understandable that historical studies were relatively meagre. But with the expansion of certificate courses to three years and with the institution in the 1960s of four-year B.Ed. courses, there is more scope for these studies and the possibility of pursuing them further in advanced courses and higher degrees.

Turning now to the fourth strand in the study of education, we have to note that, because of a revolution affecting most philosophers' conceptions of the nature of their subject, philosophy of education as described in this book is a relatively recent contribution to the study of education. For example, a pioneer book which indicates something of the nature of this contribution was C. D. Hardie's *Truth and Fallacy in Educational Theory*, first published in 1942, in which he used methods of analysis based on the work of G. E. Moore and C. D. Broad at Cambridge to assess the validity of the arguments used by some of the great educators. Professor R. S. Peters and his colleagues and ex-students at the London Institute of Education have been mainly responsible for the expansion and development of this kind of enquiry in this country.[15] It has been concerned with the analysis of the meaning of many concepts with special application to education, including 'education' itself, interest, play and development, as well as with topics equally relevant in other fields of philosophic enquiry, such as freedom, responsibility, fact, knowledge and intelligence. In sharply distinguishing this kind of enquiry from what was dealt with at an earlier date under the heading of 'Principles of Education' or the theories of the great educators already referred to, we are not asserting that these are valueless activities: what we are saying is that they are not for the most part specifically philosophic activities. As we have mentioned above, the 'First Principles' referred to in the title of Sir Percy Nunn's influential book were derived from the fields of biology and psychology. In fact, Sir Percy made valuable contributions to philosophic enquiry (he was president of the Aristotelian Society in 1925) and showed in that a capacity for rigorous analysis which is almost entirely lacking in *Education: Its Data and First Principles*. No doubt his missionary zeal to promote progressive education (much needed indeed at that time) obscured the need for philosophic rigour.[16]

Another classic in this tradition is A. N. Whitehead's *The Aims of Education*, 1929. This is a wise and witty book about educational values and the nature of the educative process. His three-phase theory of instruction will provide a better framework and guide for student teachers preparing lessons than the outmoded Herbartian stages one can still discern under the surface of many lesson notebooks. It is full of valuable insights and practical wisdom; but there is nothing distinctively philosophic about its content or mode of thought. The same comment could be made about most of the 'great educators' of the past. Either they were not in any serious sense philosophers, like Rousseau, or they were, but, like Locke, wrote about education rather as sensible, practical men of the world without relating their philosophic theories or techniques to their discussion of educational topics. John Dewey was a notable exception. He discussed educational issues in terms of his own general philosophic theories and in doing so also exemplified his own description of thinking as problem solving.

What came to be realized much more fully in the 1960s was the need, in R. S. Peters' words, to make 'a crucial distinction between the logical and psychological aspects of learning'. In the consideration of key terms for the educator, such as 'learning', 'development', 'thinking' or 'interest', 'need' and 'drive', there are psychological issues on which light can be thrown by empirical investigation. But, equally important, there are conceptual issues, what Ryle has called the 'logical geography' of the terms, which can be tackled only by using appropriate techniques of semantic and conceptual analysis. The need for this kind of analysis also arises with terms which raise ethical and social issues, such as 'authority', 'freedom', 'equality' and 'discipline'. Israel Scheffler's book *The Language of Education* (1960) gave impetus to this kind of analysis of educational terms.[17]

One further consequence of the application of analytic techniques in the field of education has been that it has led to an examination of the concept 'theory of education' and a consideration of the practical consequences of this for the study of education as carried on in colleges and departments of education.[18] What kind of a subject is 'education' in this sense of the term? That the subjects we are familiar with in the school and college curricula are not only different from each other but are also different in different ways seems self-evident. Some are different because they seem to exemplify different ways of thinking – different forms of thought with distinct logical structures. They produce different families of concepts whose relationships determine what meaningful propositions can be made, and they involve different types of testing to establish the validity of the propositions. This is not to deny that at a deeper level of cognitive activity there are general logical principles common to all these forms of thought; but certainly, above this level, if one passes from say mathematical to historical study, the differences are more apparent than the similarities. It should also be noted that within the basic forms of thought, there are subdivisions based on a particular selection of data or the use of a particular method of investigation; thus science is subdivided into physics, chemistry, biology and so on.

Some of the familiar curricular 'subjects', then, indicate these forms of knowledge or their subdivisions. But there are other 'subjects' which are not like this; they indicate rather fields of knowledge or general centres of interest which are studied by the use of a number of different basic disciplines or forms of thought. Among the traditional subjects, geography is of this kind. Physical and social sciences, mathematics and history all make contributions to the study of 'man in his environment', the central theme. The number of field subjects has grown in recent years, especially in the 'new' universities of post-war foundation, partly through the development of new subjects which straddle borderlines of older ones, partly by the deliberate relating of subjects for educational purposes, e.g. a particular period of a particular civilization may be studied in terms of its history, art, literature, science, technology, etc. It is clear that 'education' is a field subject, not a basic discipline; there is no distinctively 'educational' way of thinking; in studying education one is using psychological or historical or sociological or philosophical ways of thinking to throw light on some problem in the field of human learning. Professor Paul Hirst points to a further distinguishing feature of educational theory in that it is what he calls 'practical theory'. The main point of studying subjects like education, medicine or engineering is to throw light on or lead to applications in a field of practice:

> Thus educational theory, like all other practical theories, has a logical unity that a mere field of knowledge centred on education would not have. The unity of the theory goes beyond that of a collection of knowledge centred on some interest to that of a rational structure where knowledge from the forms provides the basis of justification for a series of educational principles.[19]

It follows from this that in courses preparing people to become teachers, engineers or doctors, the relating of theory and practice *in the course itself* has a special importance, for a failure to relate them adequately would indeed seem to contradict the nature of educational study as practical theory. The nature of this relationship is therefore considered in the chapter of this book which follows the accounts of the four main contributory disciplines.

Notes

1. R. and N. C. C. Southey, *Life of Andrew Bell*, Longman, 1844.
2. C. H. Judd, *The Training of Teachers in England, Scotland and Germany*, U.S.A. Bureau of Education, Washington, 1914.
3. L. G. E. Jones, *The Training of Teachers in England and Wales*, Milford, 1924.
4. George Collins, *Notes on School Management*, Moffatt, 1884.
5. W. S. Monroe, *Teacher-Learning Theory and Teacher Education*, Greenwood, 1952.
6. H. S. N. McFarland, *Psychology and Teaching*, Harrap, 1958.
7. Association of Teachers in Colleges, *Teaching Educational Psychology in Training Colleges*, 1962.
8. C. M. Fleming, 'The Basic Discipline', *Bulletin of Education*, No. 29, 1952.
9. J. E. Floud and A. H. Halsey, *Social Class and Educational Opportunity*, Heinemann, 1957; and B. Jackson and D. Marsden, *Education and the Working Class*, Routledge & Kegan Paul, 1962.
10. *15–18, Report of the Central Advisory Council* (Crowther Report), 1959; and *Report of the Committee on Higher Education* (Robbins Report), 1964.
11. For detailed references see W. Taylor, 'The Sociology of Education' in J. W. Tibble, ed., *The Study of Education*, 1966, pp. 211–13. A pioneer work in this field was W. Waller, *Sociology of Teaching*, Chapman & Hall, 1932.
12. In his preface to the second edition Quick says that he had had difficulty in getting the first edition published, had had to sell off 500 copies at a reduced price and that it had remained out of print for twenty years, though reprinted several times in the United States without his consent.
13. H. C. Barnard, review in *British Journal of Educational Studies*, May 1965.
14. Since 1951 the *British Journal of Educational Studies* has published a steady stream of articles and bibliographies in this field.
15. R. S. Peters, *Education as Initiation*, 1964, and *Ethics and Education*, Allen & Unwin, 1966. A Philosophy of Education Society was founded in December 1964.
16. J. W. Tibble, 'Sir Percy Nunn, 1870–1914', *British Journal of Education Studies*, November 1961.
17. R. S. Peters, ed., *The Concept of Education*, Routledge & Kegan Paul, 1967; and also R. F. Dearden, 'The Philosophy of Primary Education', in Tibble, ed., *The Study of Education*, Routledge & Kegan Paul, 1968.
18. For a fuller account of what follows see Paul H. Hirst in Tibble, ed., *The Study of Education*, ch. 2.
19. *Ibid.*, pp. 48–9.

2

Educational Psychology

D. G. Watts

Before you read on, try to say to yourself, or perhaps write down, what you think educational psychology is about. When I asked Paul, an undergraduate beginning a certificate course, he said he didn't know what to expect, but he was ready for anything. Charles, a sixth-former, said that it was 'something to do with deciding what would be the best careers for people'. Mrs Smith, who was waiting to enter a college as a mature student, thought it was 'how to deal with children, particularly difficult children'. Paul, of course, was wise, while Charles and Mrs Smith were certainly not wrong. But if you compare their reactions (and perhaps your own) with the headings in textbooks of educational psychology – 'Motivation', 'Maturation', 'Transfer of Training', 'Concept-formation' – you will see the gap which I hope this chapter will do something to close. Neither Charles nor Mrs Smith could name a single writer on educational psychology; and yet these same textbooks have lengthy index references for Sigmund Freud, Jean Piaget, B. S. Skinner, L. S. Vygotsky and many other formidable names. The intending students are not to be blamed. Educational psychology and its parent discipline psychology are not normally taught in schools (perhaps they should be), and if they are touched on in discussion periods, it is usually in the rather limited context of the emotional problems of adolescents. Similarly, an undergraduate studying geography, or history, or literature can pursue his course quite satisfactorily without reading one book on a psychological topic. And if a student *is* attracted by a paperback on a bookstall, it may contain only the kind of psychology satirized in James Thurber's *Let Your Mind Alone*.

Almost total unfamiliarity, then, is the first problem of the intending student. The second is vocabulary. Every subject has a specialized terminology, almost like a code. I cannot follow a radio commentary on a baseball game, and I am sure that baseball fans are baffled by cricket commentaries. The object of such a code is to provide a shorthand through which those interested in a subject can talk about it more rapidly and precisely than the general public. If Snow bowls an in-swinger and D'Oliveira, attempting an on-drive, is caught at short leg, ten million Englishmen know exactly the complex series of movements which have taken place. When Piaget writes a chapter on 'Assimilation, Accommodation and Organization peculiar to the Mobile Schemata', perhaps a thousand psychologists know what kind of material he is going to discuss. I shall say more about vocabulary later in the chapter. Meanwhile, I shall just repeat the very simple advice given to students reading difficult manuscripts: if it looks hopeless, don't panic; read on, and after an hour or so the gist of what the author is saying will begin to come through. By the end of your education course, you will be using some of these terms yourself without noticing it.

The third problem of the intending student that I want to mention is less obvious to him, but in fact affects what he reads and is in the long run more important. Educational psychologists are not themselves agreed on what their subject is about. That doesn't make it peculiar: no one is quite sure what history or philosophy or art is either. And it doesn't really matter. Fine work is produced in all these subjects by first-class scholars who are not sure what they are doing. The difficulties arise at a lower level. Students, quite understandably, like books called *Fundamentals of Educational Psychology* which give a smooth résumé of each of the subject's main findings with a one-page application to teaching. But even the textbooks do not hide the arguments and contradictions. Stones, for instance, has managed to write a very useful *Introduction to Educational Psychology* without mentioning Freud (but isn't Freud the most famous of all psychologists?); while Hill's widely recommended book *Learning* (1964) contains no reference to Piaget (isn't Piaget the most important theorist of learning?). When I checked the indexes of a number of books which students of education were likely to read, I found that the only two major psychologists mentioned in all of them were the Russian I. P. Pavlov, who is famous for his work with dogs, and the German W. Kohler, whose best-known work was on *The Mentality of Apes*.

The fact is that psychology is not a discipline like an army unit, in which individual psychologists belong to well-ordered platoons, the platoons to companies, and the companies to battalions, all working together to a common plan. It better resembles a fun-fair, with animal trainers, fortune tellers, memory men, card sharpers, bearded ladies and others, functioning on their own in badly-lit tents. Not every visitor to the fairground finds every booth to his taste: we all make a different choice of amusements; but nevertheless we come away from the fairground stimulated and with our curiosity aroused. This is the spirit in which this chapter recommends the beginning student to approach the diverse field of educational psychology. Let us look then at what happens in some of the tents on the fairground.

Galton

Francis Galton (died 1911) was Charles Darwin's half-cousin, a remarkable scholar and an ingenious investigator. In 1880 he sent out by post one of the earliest questionnaires, in which he asked people if they could recall the image, or the appearance, of their breakfast table that morning (try it yourself). The replies showed remarkable differences: some people could remember every detail of colour and shape, even the sparkling of glass, reflections and shadows; others, though they knew what they had had for breakfast, were unable to visualize the scene at all. Unexpectedly, Galton's distinguished scientific acquaintances turned out to have much less ability in this field than many ordinary people. And perhaps more significant, it was found that poor visualizers just would not believe that other people did have images of this kind, while good visualizers assumed that everybody else 'thought' in just the same way as they did themselves. Evidence like this encouraged Galton's successors, among other things, to try to describe and measure differences between people.

Freud

When, early in his career, Sigmund Freud (died 1939) was working with Josef Breuer, another distinguished Viennese doctor, he encountered the now famous case of Anna O, aged twenty-one. Anna was sent to Breuer for treatment for a nervous cough, but in fact displayed an extraordinary variety of symptoms. Although a German, she appeared to be able to speak only in English and automatically translated any writing she was given in several other languages into English. She moved between a normal personality and that of a naughty little girl; and she suffered from paralysis in several limbs. Breuer visited Anna every evening, and they found that after she had talked about one of the symptoms, it was apt to disappear: Anna called this 'the talking cure' or 'chimney sweeping'. After a while, Breuer concluded that Anna's symptoms were associated with incidents at her father's death-bed. Freud went on, on the basis of cases like this, to develop the technique of psycho-analysis and to elaborate his ingenious theories about the human personality. His work has had a profound effect on our attitudes to children and their behaviour.

Pavlov

I. P. Pavlov (died 1936) was a Russian doctor who began using dogs in his work on the digestion of food. He noticed that a dog produced saliva in its mouth not only when it was given food, but also when it saw the dish, and even when it heard the footsteps of its handler in the corridor. As an experiment, Pavlov then began to sound a buzzer every time the dog was fed. After a while, he found that the dog could be made to salivate merely by sounding the buzzer, when there was no sign of feeding. The dog could do something new: it had 'learned' in this simple way to react to the buzzer. Pavlov went on to 'condition' dogs in many other ways. Some psychologists came to think that this was the basic form of learning and that all learning, in human beings as well as in animals, might be merely a highly complicated version of the kind of learning which Pavlov had demonstrated in dogs.

Thorndike and Skinner

The American E. L. Thorndike (died 1949) devised a 'problem box' with which he experimented with cats. The 'box' was a cage with a door which could be opened by pulling on a looped string inside the cage. Hungry cats were put inside the cage, and in the course of scratching about they pulled the string and let themselves out to food outside. The more often they were put in the box, the quicker they discovered the effect of pulling the string, until they pulled the string as soon as the door was closed. B. F. Skinner (born 1904) developed the ideas suggested by the work of Pavlov and Thorndike. His 'Skinner box' basically has a lever which, when pressed, releases a quantity of food into a bowl. Using this box, Skinner has done an enormous number of experiments on the learning of rats and pigeons. He and other psychologists have also made extensive use of small mazes to find out how quickly and in what way rats and other animals learn to choose the right route. On the basis of these and other observations, Skinner and others have devised a 'learning theory' which they believe applies to human as well as animal learning.

Kohler

Wolfgang Kohler (died 1967) was a German psychologist who was interned on the island of Tenerife during the First World War and was able to observe and experiment with the chimpanzees there. He showed how chimpanzees could fit two sticks together to pull in a banana which was out of their reach and could pile several boxes on top of one another to reach a high banana. More important, the chimpanzees appeared to learn how to solve these problems not by trial-and-error like Thorndike's cats, but by suddenly getting up and doing them, as though they had 'seen' the whole solution in their heads. Kohler and other 'gestalt' psychologists (from a German word for 'shape' or 'form' of thought) believed that this was evidence of the way in which human beings think, not in many small steps, like Pavlov's dogs and Skinner's rats, but by seeing a pattern in a situation.

Piaget

Jean Piaget (born 1896), a Swiss psychologist, has made lengthy and detailed observations of children, including his own, from birth to adolescence. He noticed, for instance, that very young babies may follow with their eyes a parent walking across the room, but if the parent walks behind a screen, the baby stops looking. When it is a little older, however, the baby's eyes go on across the screen, expecting the parent to reappear on the other side. With children of five and six his most famous experiment has been on 'conservation'. The children he tested believed that there was more water in a tall thin container than in a short fat container, even when the same quantity of water was poured from one to another, and that when a ball of plasticine was rolled out into a sausage shape it had more plasticine in it. Piaget shows how differently children think from adults and how slowly they learn. On the basis of his observations, he has developed an elaborate theory of learning quite different from that of Skinner.

Bruner

J. S. Bruner is a professor at Harvard University who has made an important contribution to curriculum theory (see below) and to several aspects of psychology. He has, for instance, suggested a different interpretation from Piaget's for the results of experiments with children on 'conservation'. But perhaps he and his collaborators are best known for their book *A Study of Thinking*, which includes accounts of experiments, with Harvard students as subjects, on 'concept attainment' and 'categorizing'. The experimenters worked with sets of cards marked with various signs, for example squares, circles or crosses, each of which could be black, red or green, and could be in ones, twos or threes. The experimenter decided on a category, say cards with one red circle, but did not tell the subject what it was. The subject turned over one card at a time, and the experimenter said 'yes' if the card had any of the attributes of the chosen category, that is a single figure, a circle or the colour red. The subject's task was to work out from the answers what category the experimenter had in mind. Bruner found that different subjects used very different methods or 'strategies' in tackling such problems. He called the strategies used in one test 'simultaneous-scanning', 'successive-scanning', 'conservative-focusing' and 'focus-gambling'. He and his colleagues hoped that an analysis of the mental strategies used in tests like these would tell them something about the basic ways in which the mind is organized to deal with information and problems.

Cattell

R. B. Cattell (born 1905) is an Englishman, from Devon, who is a professor at the University of Illinois. His main interest has been in the construction of questionnaires and tests designed to reveal basic characteristics of people's personalities. In one test he and a colleague compared the scores of 600 American students with those of 200 British undergraduates and technical students. They believed that the findings showed that British students were less anxious, more introverted, more sensitive and more radical; whereas the American students were more anxious, more extraverted, less sensitive and more conservative. It has been suggested that the differences of personality among schoolchildren shown by tests like these could form a more sensible basis for streaming or grouping children than the intelligence and attainment tests used for this purpose at present.

Lippitt and White

Perhaps the best known of all experiments in the field of social psychology have been those of the Americans R. Lippitt and R. K. White with members of a boys' club. The boys were divided into four groups, and each of the groups was at various times given three different kinds of leadership: authoritarian, *laissez-faire* and democratic. The authoritarian leader directed the boys and told them what to do; the *laissez-faire* leader sat around and did nothing; the democratic leader discussed what to do with the boys. It was found that when the authoritarian leader was in the room some of the group were rebellious and others cowed; when he left the room, they let themselves go. With the *laissez-faire* leader, the boys were frustrated and bewildered. With the democratic leader, the boys not only got on with their work, but they went on working when he left the room. There seems to be a straightforward lesson in this for teachers; but the conditions and methods of the experiment have been criticized, and it needs to be repeated on a larger scale.

Hudson

Liam Hudson, a professor at Edinburgh University, has considered the question of how people think in quite a different way from Bruner. Hudson has tested boys at grammar and public schools and then followed up their careers at various universities. One of his tests is called 'Uses of Objects'. When asked to describe the uses of a barrel and a blanket, Poulter, a young scientist, wrote: (Barrel) 'Container for liquids. Sitting on'; (Blanket) 'Sleeping in'.

Bolton, a young linguist at the same school, wrote: (Barrel) 'Storing beer; sitting on; using as a raft; gnawing; loud-speaker holder; as a musical instrument'; (Blanket) 'Sleeping in; using to stifle burning; keep warm; lag pipes; round a camp fire; suffocating people; muffler and insulator for sound; for clothes'. Hudson has called people who think like Poulter 'convergers', and people who think like Bolton 'divergers'. He has been interested in what aspects of people's personalities cause them to think in the ways they do and in what effect these ways of thinking have on people's success in various academic subjects.

Education and psychology

Now that we have looked at some of the things psychologists do, we can say rather more generally what the subject is about. Educational psychology tries to use the methods and findings of psychology to understand the process of education, and where possible to improve the practice of education. But psychology offers no easy answers to classroom problems. Some applications of psychological ideas in the classroom are extremely controversial: two examples are the relaxation of discipline in 'progressive' schools and the use of intelligence tests in selection. In other cases, though we can see the importance of a piece of research, we have to recognize that years of curriculum development may be needed before the findings can usefully be put into practice. However, it is important that we should try to understand our problems better, even if at the moment we cannot solve them; and though there may be no magic formula for educational success, we may find ourselves making a few modest improvements in our schools.

By 'education' we mean, of course, the whole educational system, and not just school-teaching. The educational psychologist is directly concerned with the problems and abnormalities of children and the services provided to deal with them; Valentine's book *The Normal Child and Some of his Abnormalities* is a useful introduction to this field. The psychologist is also interested in play-groups and nurseries and, like Freud and Piaget, pays a great deal of attention to the child's experience before coming to school. He works, as does Hudson, not only in junior but in secondary, grammar, and public schools; and like Cattell and Bruner, with students in higher and adult education as well as children. He investigates the psychology of the classroom, the psychology of the staffroom, of the headmaster's study and the offices at County Hall. Tests, examinations, classroom materials, textbooks and school design are all within his field of study. He may find it necessary in explaining what happens in the school to consider the psychology of parents and employers, of teenage groups and the pop culture, of races and social classes.

When you take a particular education course, your lecturers may quite properly decide to concentrate their attention on the problems most relevant to you. But don't misunderstand this and suppose that educational psychology is only about the language development of infants, or 'conservation' in lower juniors, or intelligence tests for eleven-year-olds; it is about those things, but it can be interesting and instructive about a great many other topics as well.

Psychology and 'behaviour'

We can now go on to discuss some of the difficult vocabulary of psychology and, in explaining it, to introduce the areas of study with which the words are associated. I shall begin with 'psychology' itself and with 'behaviour', which has a psychological meaning very different from that of a child's 'bad behaviour'.

Old-fashioned dictionaries define psychology as the study, or science, of the mind. But many psychologists are of the opinion that we know so little about the 'mind' that the definition is meaningless. Some, indeed, believe that the popular use of the word 'mind' is on the same level as the use of words like 'ghost' or 'fairy'. Introspection, or looking into our own 'mind' and claiming that it exists, is something which cannot be checked by anyone else and is therefore no more scientific than claiming that we have seen fairies. Psychologists who take this view use the word 'mentalistic' as a critical description of colleagues whose work they regard as old-fashioned and unsound.

More modern definitions of 'psychology' try to begin from the actions which we can observe a person or an animal performing, his 'behaviour'. In particular, psychologists are interested in behaviour which is in some sense chosen by an animal. Even very primitive animals like jelly-fish choose whether to move towards light or away from it, towards or away from food. Can we give a scientific explanation of the process of choice, whether it is the simple behaviour of the jelly-fish or the highly complex behaviour of a human being?

'Behaviourist' psychologists like Thorndike and Skinner believe that all animal choices are best explained in terms of the simple, mindless jelly-fish, that is in terms of the animal's *response* (in this case, movement) to a *stimulus* (light). They express this in the code S-R. Even human behaviour, then, is made up of sets of stored or conditioned responses, complex versions of the responses of Pavlov's dogs, which lead from stimuli to responses by the chain reaction of series of S-R connections. Theories of this kind are, indeed, sometimes called 'connectionist'. In such an analysis there is no need to suppose that the animal (or person) decides or 'thinks' at all. Because it is based only on the observable and measurable behaviour of animals, behaviourist psychologists have claimed that theirs is the truly scientific learning theory. Some, like the American Clark Hull, even hoped that the ways in which S-R connections were put together to make up complex behaviour might in time be described in mathematical formulae, which could then be used to predict behaviour.

Other psychologists, working from a behaviourist point-of-view, have decided that it may be simpler to suppose that something happens 'inside' the animal between the stimulus and the response, which might be called 'mediating processes' or a central processing mechanism; and the amateur may be excused for thinking that this is the 'mind' after all. Students interested in these problems can go on to read chapter 12 in Wright's *Introducing Psychology*. Whichever view we may take though, it is advisable to be careful when using words like 'mental' and 'mind' in your essays. To some students, behaviourist learning theory may seem cold and heartless. Whatever its general validity, however, in some fields, as Gagné's *The Conditions of Learning* shows, it has produced some very practical suggestions for more effective teaching.

Neurophysiology

Quite a different approach to explaining the behaviour of human beings and animals is that of physiology and neurophysiology, the study not so much of the observed behaviour of animals, but of the physical structures by which they respond to stimuli. The physiologist is interested in the brain, the glands and the nervous system, and in the chemical, physical and electrical processes which take place in animal behaviour. Hitherto, this work has been most valuable to education in the diagnosis and treatment of abnormalities in children. But in future it promises to give us a systematic account of the physical basis of children's personalities and abilities – scientific in another sense to that of the behaviourists. The book in this field which has most influenced educationists has been the Canadian D. O. Hebb's *The Organization of Behaviour*. The account he gives there of the development of the brain during learning, and his distinction between the capacity of the brain (intelligence A) and the way in which it is developed by experience (intelligence B), has made an important contribution to the arguments about the effect of teaching on children's abilities. Hebb has also written a very sound *Textbook of Psychology*. W. Grey Walter's book *The Living Brain*, written in a popular style, provides an interesting account of Walter's own work with recording by electroencephalogram (E.E.G.) the electrical activity of the brain and also serves as an introduction to modern work on the mechanical simulation of 'mental' processes.

Ethology

Animal experiments, especially with rats and pigeons, were once particularly associated with the behaviourist psychologists, but in the past twenty years the increasing amount of work on the behaviour of animals, both in captivity and in the field, has led to the coining of a new name, 'ethology'. The great visual interest of animal behaviour has made this a deservedly popular television subject. I shall only mention two areas of research which seem to be relevant to human learning. Tinbergen's work on the way herring gull chicks recognize a red spot on the adult's beak and then learn to feed has given us some new clues to the relationship between 'innate' (inborn, inherited) behaviour and learned behaviour in young animals. The moving accounts of the Harlows' work with young rhesus monkeys, particularly on their attachment to 'cloth mothers', have thrown light on the same subject and at the same time have suggested parallels with the origins of emotional disturbances in human children. Barnett's *Instinct and Intelligence* is a very readable introduction to this field.

Perception

The response of chicks to the sight of a beak and of monkeys to the feel of hair are evidence of innate *perception*. But in fact, young animals appear to display only a limited number of innate perceptual responses. In general, we have to learn how to see and hear what psychologists would call our *environment*, the things outside ourselves. The problem of how we do this has concerned philosophers and psychologists for centuries. For in deciding what the things in our environment are, we each have only our interpretation of the evidence from our fallible senses to go on. Animals like bats and dogs see or hear things differently from human beings; even adult human beings can differ in what they believe they experience, as Galton's investigations demonstrated; and many of Piaget's observations show that children see things very differently from adults. In the school, children are not just learning facts: they are also still learning to recognize shapes and sounds, and to distinguish, or *discriminate*, them as adults do. It would be possible for a teacher to give a child a problem which he might be able to *do*, but which he was unable to *see*. This is true both in the infant school, where Piaget suggests, for instance, that children just cannot *see* different kinds of flowers, and in higher education, where a lecturer may point out re-entrants or Perpendicular windows which his less experienced students *know about* but cannot really *see*.

The topic of perception is at present a relatively neglected one in educational discussion, partly because gestalt psychology, which was very concerned with perception, is now unfashionable. But students of art in particular may like to read *Visual Thinking*, written by Rudolf Arnheim from a gestalt point-of-view. Some interesting observations on the perceptual elements in the teaching of medical students are made by Mrs Abercrombie in *The Anatomy of Judgement*. Gregory's *Eye and Brain* gives a good general introduction to the subject.

Freud and the emotions

I used the word 'emotional' when talking about the Harlows' monkeys, but as with words like 'mind', 'behaviour' and 'thinking', 'emotion' in a psychological sense may not mean quite what it does in ordinary conversation. Some writers use another word, 'affect', as almost synonymous with 'emotion' and talk about 'affective states' rather than 'emotions'. If we want to make a distinction, we could say that 'emotion' is the roused-up state, such as anger or fear, itself, while 'affect' is an idea or state-of-mind influenced by emotion, like fear of heights. You must distinguish, of course, between the normal use of the word 'affection' for a loving feeling and 'affect' used in this way.

It would be impossible to summarize here the enormous psychological literature on the emotional aspects of human behaviour. Indeed, many people believe that this is what psychology is all about. Freud is by no means the only writer on the subject, but his brilliant theories, evolved to explain cases like Anna O's, suggested powerfully that human personality and behaviour were the outcome of the ways in which we try to regulate certain instincts, 'drives' and emotional states. Freud's ideas have, perhaps justifiably, been criticized as untestable speculation, but he has had more impact on popular thinking than any other psychological writer. And as applied to children by Melanie Klein, Susan Isaacs and his own daughter Anna, his ideas have been just as influential in education. When added to the influence of John Dewey and the earlier writers Froebel and Pestalozzi, they probably tipped the scale in the middle years of this century away from the older, authoritarian, didactic school regime to the freer, more sympathetic atmosphere of today. This newer atmosphere was designed both to allow for the child's affective development within the school and to recognize the role which the child's needs and interests play in making him willing – motivating him – to learn. Not all teachers and parents, of course, agree with these 'progressive' ideas, and some educationists too are very critical.

Stafford Clark's *What Freud Really Said* will introduce you to the special vocabulary of Freudian psychology, and you should try to read Ernest Jones' excellent biography of Freud.

Personality

In popular usage the word 'personality' has in recent years shifted from its meaning in expressions like 'gloomy personality' or 'cheerful personality' to *having* 'personality' (some kind of striking and attractive characteristic) and even *being* 'a personality' (someone well-known and publicized). Psychologists use the word in the older sense, as the collection of characteristics or traits which seem in normal human beings to be integrated to produce the coherent and predictable behaviour of 'John Smith' or 'you' or 'myself' (though in abnormal states, people like Anna O may have dual or even multiple personalities). The traits of personality may include inherited characteristics, emotional or affective states, ways of thinking, beliefs and opinions.

We can distinguish two general approaches to the understanding of personality. In that taken, for instance, by Freud and his contemporaries Adler and Jung, some central trait of character, such as an 'inferiority complex' or 'intraversion' is postulated on the basis of observation, and the rest of the individual's personality and behaviour interpreted by reference to it. The more modern approach, used by Cattell in America and H. J. Eysenck in Britain, is to establish what are the more fundamental traits of personality by means of tests and questionnaires given to large numbers of people and the mathematical analysis of their results. The findings are used to construct increasingly reliable tests for individuals. Such tests, as our sixth-former Charles knew, can then be employed, for instance, in vocational guidance and selection, or to diagnose maladjustment and learning difficulties. Cattell gives a lively account of his work in *The Scientific Analysis of Personality* (notice the word 'scientific' again), but his confidence in its future usefulness has not quite been justified in recent years.

Child development

'Child development' is the term used for the systematic study of the growth and maturation of children, including their physical growth, emotional, perceptual and intellectual development, personality, and social development. Its psychological aspects may be referred to as child psychology, developmental psychology or genetic psychology (a confusing usage, because it is not connected with the biological word 'gene'). Work in this field has often taken the form of patient and detailed observation of individuals and groups, such as that done by Arnold Gesell in America, Charlotte Buhler in Germany and Susan Isaacs in Britain; Piaget's research, though it has much wider objectives, has also been a major contribution to the study of child development. Textbooks reporting such work frequently set out their findings in the form of summaries of the characteristics and typical behaviour of children at various ages. This is certainly helpful for students specializing in the teaching of particular age-ranges, and some college courses in psychology also once took this form. But in recent years this approach has fallen out of favour. The range and sophistication of educational research makes it increasingly difficult to take a research finding and put it into a generalized picture of a child without explaining the theory and methods of the researcher. Piaget's experiments, for instance, are very widely quoted without reference to their theoretical context. A more modern approach would be to take a particular aspect of a child's development, such as speech, and to consider the research appropriate to it. But the works of Gesell and his collaborators, such as *Youth: the Years from Ten to Sixteen*, still remain fascinating reading.

Thinking and cognition

Up to now I have not discussed some activities which many people would regard as the ones with which education is most concerned – knowing, thinking and reasoning. Psychologists group these, with perception, as 'cognition' and talk about the 'cognitive' rather than the intellectual development of children. A few moments' introspection by the reader will make it clear how many difficult questions there are in this field. Are you 'thinking' while you are reading? Do you think in words? Do you talk silently to yourself while you think? Can you think in images like Galton's acquaintances? When you hit a difficult return at tennis, to what extent has your nervous system 'thought the problem out'? If there were a sudden explosion outside the room, would you 'think' about your reactions?

As we have seen, some behaviourist psychologists doubt whether, since we cannot observe them, it is useful to talk about such processes at all, and their 'connectionist' theories are contrasted with 'cognitive' theories. Cognitive theorists start with the presumption that human beings have some kind of central processing mechanism which is responsible for what are called knowing and thinking, and try to devise experiments to show how at least part of that mechanism works. The gestalt psychologists are cognitive theorists (Kohler believed that the behaviour of his chimpanzees was evidence of 'insight'); but they differ from other psychologists in thinking that we are physically equipped with patterns of perceiving and knowing (*gestalten*), and that cognitive development consists of using those patterns in explaining our experience. Piaget too is a cognitive theorist. His detailed observations are not primarily intended to give information about children, but are only part of the evidence he has amassed to support a monumental theory about human thought. Unlike some gestalt writers, he does not believe that we are born with a rudimentary 'mind', any more than our ape ancestors had a human mind; he thinks that we evolve our mind in the course of growing up, just as homo sapiens evolved it historically. Further, he thinks that he can show that the mind learns to operate through certain logical and mathematical rules, or 'operations'. Bruner is another cognitive theorist. He has also evolved a theory for the cognitive development of children, though a less ambitious one than Piaget's, but, as we have seen, he is particularly interested in the ways in which adults use certain schemes or 'strategies' for the solution of problems. We could say that '*gestalten*', 'operations' and 'strategies' are all words which attempt to describe the processes through which human beings organize their responses to stimuli more effectively than lower animals. You can take up some of these points in chapter 16 of Wright's *Introducing Psychology*.

Concepts, schema and transfer-of-training

You will often meet the words 'concept' and 'schema' (plural: 'schemata') in writing about cognition. They are not always used in the same way, but we must attempt a definition. The words describe cognitive structures which operate at a lower level than 'operations' or 'strategies', but which have the same function of simplifying and arranging information so that it can be handled more effectively. Concepts are what might once have been called 'ideas', that is, notions which are more general than individual instances of a case: for instance, 'tree' represents something other than any observable trees; 'liquid' is a concept distinct from any particular material; 'imagination', from any example of imagining. Learning or acquiring concepts obviously simplifies the way we see and think about the world. Once a child can distinguish the concept 'Daddy' from the concept 'man' he has a clearer understanding of his social environment. Much formal learning is in fact the learning of concepts – 'multiplication', 'Stone Age', 'invertebrate' and 'hanging valley' are all concepts – and any light which cognitive theorists can throw on concept-formation will be very valuable for the teacher.

Schemata are plans of action, or cognitive 'maps', which guide responses to whole sets of circumstances and are sufficiently general to accommodate most of the novel situations we encounter. A simple example is opening a door in a strange room. Whatever their shape, size and colour, we recognize the concepts 'door' and 'handle', and without 'thinking' we proceed in a smooth series of actions, which involve assumptions about space, time and movement, to open it. When it turns out to be a sliding, not a hinged door, a person of average intelligence can still rapidly adjust to the situation. We have employed a series of perceptual (recognizing the situation), sensori-motor (feeling and moving) and cognitive (knowing what to do) schemata. If you think about your own daily life, say eating breakfast or jumping on a bus, you will see that for much of the time you are not 'thinking', but applying schemata, rather as an aeroplane flies on an automatic pilot. One difference between a learner and an expert in any field clearly lies in the smooth application of relevant schemata.

Cognitive structures of this kind also contribute to the phenomenon called 'transfer' or 'transfer-of-training'. It has long been noticed that once a person has learned to solve one kind of problem, he appears to be able to solve other kinds of problems of equal difficulty rather more quickly. He has learned not just the way to do a particular thing, but some sort of rule for tackling problems. This is very important for teachers, who cannot possibly teach children how to deal with all the problems they will encounter and who in fact teach a certain amount of material in the hope that it is a good training, that is, it will transfer to as many situations as possible. Some teachers think their own school subject is a good training of this kind, but their evidence for this is only a mixture of prejudice and guesswork. Research on cognitive processes may one day give us more reliable guidance on the most useful subjects and material to teach. One reason why many people are excited by Piaget's work is that they think he has given us a 'scientific' account of the basic processes on which learning is based.

More about Piaget

Let us say a little more then about Piaget's account of the child's development. He sees the development of intelligence in terms of three broad stages: a sensori-motor and pre-operational stage from infancy to age 7–8; one of *concrete operations* to age 12–13; and one of *formal operations* from about age 13 onwards. The infant develops schemata *about* its feelings and movements *by* feeling and moving; he comes to perform the complex activities, for instance, of walking and opening doors. But he cannot apply or transfer these schemata to other situations involving similar principles. After age 7–8, he can do this; for instance, he can think in a general way about the movement of hinges and pivots, but only by using actual hinges or models of them, or perhaps by considering mental images of them. In his conceptual development, the infant learns concepts by doing (say, running) or by handling (say, a ball), and then identifies the words which adults use to represent the concepts. The practical recommendation for the school is that the child must be allowed to pour water, dig sand, use different lengths of wood *before* we begin to talk to him about capacity, weight, length or whatever concept we are concerned with. Only after age 12–13 can we safely begin to talk to children in terms of abstract concepts. You can go on reading about Piaget in Wright's *Introducing Psychology*, chapter 18. After that, try Boyle's *Student's Guide to Piaget*, leaving out the very theoretical first chapter. But enough has probably already been said to indicate that by no means all psychologists agree with the conclusions Piaget has reached.

Language

A field in which there have been important modern developments that to some extent run counter to Piagetian theory is the study of language, that is, one's native tongue rather than foreign languages. It parallels in psychology the work of Bernstein in sociology (see below). It is easy for adults to forget what an important and sophisticated achievement is the learning of language by young children. Children have first a major perceptual task in discriminating and identifying the sounds made by adults; they have to learn the difficult sensori-motor activities required to produce matching sounds; they have to learn the complex code which sounds form in making a language; and they have to learn that words are not just labels for objects, but concepts referring to classes of activities and objects. As we have seen, Piaget thinks that action must precede conceptualization. But other writers, including the Russian L. S. Vygotsky, see the child as acquiring a word, and with the word a vague concept, and then gradually finding how the word fits his experience to make a concept; so that in Vygotsky's classroom, the teacher would talk more, he would encourage the children to talk more, and there would be more reading and writing, than in Piaget's classroom. Bruner and the Russian A. R. Luria are other writers who have emphasized the importance of language in the child's development. In general, there is a strong modern trend towards encouraging children throughout school life to talk to the teacher, to one another and to the general public, both to improve their skill in communication and to encourage the conceptual development which lies behind it. Stones' *Introduction to Educational Psychology* has two useful chapters on language; and Mrs Abercrombie's book, already mentioned, describes how she has used the discussion method with students.

Intelligence and testing

In popular speech we use the words 'intelligent' and 'intelligence' to describe some kind of overall ability for dealing with situations of many kinds. A highly intelligent pupil may get good O and A level results in all the subjects he takes and then go on to get First Class degrees in two different university faculties. What I have said about cognitive structures, and their function as systems for dealing with diverse information, may suggest that there is indeed some ultimate cognitive structure which can analyse the common factors in all situations and which results in 'intelligent' behaviour. Intelligence testing has tried to find this factor in human abilities, not in the manner of Piaget by prolonged personal observation, but like the personality analysts, by large-scale testing, measurement and mathematical analysis. Beginning with simple tests devised by the Frenchman Alfred Binet to distinguish subnormal children, psychologists like the Americans Terman and Merrill and the Englishman Burt gradually elaborated tests and questionnaires which gave consistent results when applied to large numbers of people. The tests appeared to be able to distinguish not only subnormal and normal children, but a finely graded rank-order of ability which could be expressed as the 'intelligence quotient'. Many testers believed that they could show by mathematical analysis that people's scores were not just the result of separate abilities – knowing things or being quick at figures or good with words – but were the outcome of a single thread of ability running through all the answers, which might reasonably be called intelligence. This ability then seemed to correlate very well with success in school and in employment. Like the Piagetians today, some testers were very excited by their findings. They thought that their methods gave the findings a scientific objectivity which few, if any, other branches of psychology could claim. The work of schools too could be put on a much sounder footing. Difficulties of understanding could be quickly identified. The teacher would no longer have to rely on his impressions of who were the bright and dull children. Bright children could be put into classes where they could learn difficult material; dull children into other classes where they could learn material suited to their abilities. The case was persuasive enough to be embodied in public educational policy in England, streaming, the scholarship or 11+ examinations, tripartite secondary education and selective higher education being justified by reference to the findings of tests. In colleges, some lecturers were so enthusiastic that for a time courses were not in fact in psychology, but in testing and measurement; and you find that some older textbooks still have unexpectedly long chapters on the subject.

There is no space here to review all the criticisms of the use of intelligence tests which have been made in the past twenty years. Some readers will be familiar, for instance, with the fierce arguments which have raged around the views of the American tester Arthur Jensen. We still use intelligence tests, of course, but it is probably fair to say that to many educationists, several of the other lines of enquiry described in this chapter have come to seem more promising and fruitful. A thorough account of the history and techniques of testing is given in chapter 3 of Lovell's *Educational Psychology and Children*.

Imagination and creativity

The behaviourists, the cognitive theorists and the intelligence testers all give useful descriptions of some aspects of intelligent behaviour. But other writers have suggested that they do not adequately account for the sophisticated human activities involved in literature, drama, music and the visual arts. To the gestalt psychologists, these activities are related to our perception of form and shape; the Freudians offer explanations in terms of what they call sublimation and symbolization. Some psychologists, following Galton, have drawn attention to the great range of 'mental' activities which cannot be described in the same way as rational behaviour, for instance dreams, day-dreams, synaesthesia, eidetic images and drug-induced illusions. We seem to be in a difficult area between perception and cognition. In one direction, these phenomena merge into forms of mental illness. In another, they probably give us some clues to the way in which artists work and to the response of the audience to an artistic production.

An interesting suggestion, which has been increasingly explored in the past twenty years, is that there may be a link between imaginative activity and effective thinking. The suggestion arose partly from criticisms of intelligence tests. There often seemed to be groups of children in schools who were lively and interesting but performed poorly in tests, and some tests on successful adults also gave puzzlingly disappointing results. On the other hand, there were occasions when carefully selected groups of highly intelligent men failed to produce adequate policies: certain defects in the American space programme were cited as examples. Then, some notably effective thinkers like Darwin and Churchill had been very undistinguished at school. And the accounts which some of the best scientists and mathematicians gave of their work showed that they worked more like poets and artists than logicians. All this suggested that, though the reasoning abilities and logical intelligence measured by the existing tests had something to do with effective thinking, there were other factors not being adequately tested. Various names were given to these factors – 'divergence', 'intuition', 'originality' – but the one now most commonly used is 'creativity'.

A more systematic approach to creativity began with the American J. P. Guilford's presidential address to the American Psychological Association in 1950. Guilford and his colleagues attempted, on the basis of exhaustive tests with American officer cadets, to distinguish 120 abilities rather than one. In 1962 the Americans Getzels and Jackson, in a book called *Creativity and Intelligence*, claimed that from their work with children at a secondary school they could distinguish effective creative thinkers from effective intelligent thinkers. Getzels and Jackson's statistical findings have since been criticized, but two more Americans,

Wallach and Kogan, do seem to have established the distinction in their work with 10–11 year olds. In Britain, as we have seen, Hudson has done parallel work with public-schoolboys and undergraduates, using the terminology 'convergent/divergent'.

Critics of the idea of 'creativity' tend to regard its advocates as well-meaning but woolly enthusiasts, and research in this field certainly still has a long way to go. But the work has come as a timely warning not to allow the cognitive theorists to persuade us to concentrate on the development of logical abilities to the exclusion of colourful and imaginative material in the school. And it has reminded us to look carefully at the child in the class who is not doing quite as well at the usual exercises as we might expect, and to see if his talent in fact lies in more imaginative fields. Butcher gives a balanced review of work on creativity in his book *Human Intelligence*, chapter 4.

Social psychology and social factors

The line between social psychology and sociology is very difficult to draw, and the same pieces of research may be quoted in books on both subjects. Both consider human beings as members of groups (of two or more people), but social psychology is more interested in the effect of membership of a group on the individuals which make it up, while sociologists are more interested in the organization and functioning of the whole group. The relevance of social psychology to the school is immediately obvious: children and children, teachers and children, and teachers and teachers form close-knit groups with a strong influence on each other's behaviour. And all these people are also influenced by their membership of larger social groupings: society itself, neighbourhoods, communities, social classes, races and religions. Sprott's *Human Groups* is a readable introduction to the field.

Social psychology, like psychology, has its own terminology: the study of groups for instance is sometimes called group dynamics. A characteristic concept of social psychologists is that of 'role'. Role-theory seeks to describe people's behaviour not in terms of some inner personality, but in terms of their response to what other people expect of them – their 'role-expectations'. If you are a daughter, for example, all kinds of people expect you to behave in certain ways as a daughter – your father, your mother, other relations, the neighbours and so on (they are called the 'role-set') – and to a considerable extent you do behave as the kind of daughter they expect. The teacher's role is a particularly interesting one to analyse; many people – the children, the other teachers, the headteacher, the general public – have strong opinions on how teachers should behave, and the teacher inevitably responds to these expectations. But of course, he is expecting *them* to behave in certain ways as well. 'Role', like 'concept', is a good example of a theoretical idea which starts you thinking.

In the past twenty years there has been an increasing emphasis on the social factors in other aspects of psychology – in cognitive development, for instance, and the learning of language. This tendency has also shown itself in the criticism of theories which are based on non-social factors in development. The debate about 'intelligence' is largely about the relative effectiveness of innate factors and learned, social factors on the ability to perform well in tests. In Piaget's case, it is the weight given by his theories not to innate, but to non-social environmental factors which is criticized. The critics suggest that the child learns more from watching and listening to adults and other children than Piaget allows. In general, the concept of maturation, the steady unfolding of the child's personality and abilities with his physical growth, has to some extent been replaced by the idea of the child's development being goaded and directed by social life.

Conclusion

This chapter has tried to introduce you to some (but not all) of the writers whose work has been most influential in educational psychology, to some of the principal themes they have considered and to some of the vocabulary they use. Something has been said of the way in which psychological findings have been, or could be, applied in the schools, but I have tried to avoid giving the impression that these findings solve any of the ancient problems of teaching and learning. I have deliberately included, in nearly every section, a sentence or two of criticism: not for ill-considered insertion in 'Write a critical account of . . .' essays, but to warn the beginning student against uncritical adulation of famous names. Some of the remarkable acts in the psychological fairground do indeed need to be watched very carefully.

Read as many books as you have time for: follow up what most interests you; make up your own mind; don't worry about the parts which seem unintelligible. If, in a year or two, you can say that you are a little more aware of the implications of what you are doing and a little more sensitive to the problems of education, your course will have been worthwhile.

Further reading

One or two books have been mentioned in each section of this chapter, and these are all listed below. You can follow them up by looking at their bibliographies and, if you have access to a good library, at some of the articles in periodicals which they mention. Even if the book or article which has taken your fancy sounds very obscure, it is still worth asking your librarian whether he can get hold of it for you.

But for those who may find it useful, I am also going to recommend an old-fashioned course of reading, a number of items (thirteen in fact) to be read one after another, which you should be able to finish in a long summer holiday. The course will work on the principle of reading around the subject for a week or two, and then from time to time channelling your interest with a textbook.

Begin by borrowing from a library Gesell's *Youth: the Years from Ten to Sixteen*; read some of the pages on sixteen-year-olds, and see if you agree with his description of that age. If you know a younger child, look up his age in the same way in Gesell's *Child Development* (two volumes). Now go on to Hudson's *Contrary Imaginations*, and read chapters 2–5; decide whether you are a converger or a diverger. Then turn to the behaviour of animals, as described in Barnett's *Instinct and Intelligence*.

Return to human beings, this time to a remarkable individual, the Russian memory man Shereshevskii in Luria's *The Mind of the Mnemonist* (borrow it from your library). Shereshevskii used perceptual images in his memorizing; and you can follow up perception in Mrs Abercrombie's *The Anatomy of Judgement*. Now see how perception fits into a general picture of the subject in Adcock's straightforward textbook *Fundamentals of Psychology*. Start relating your reading to education with Bruner's short book *The Process of Education* (also relevant to curriculum theory). Then go back to another remarkable individual, this time Freud himself, in the abridged edition of Jones' *Life and Work of Sigmund Freud*. After that, try an introductory textbook not on individuals but on the behaviour of people in groups, Sprott's *Human Groups*.

Change your theme again with Walter's cheery introduction to neurophysiology *The Living Brain*. Then go back to the less easily explained aspects of the human 'mind' by reading McKellar's interesting *Experience and Behaviour*. Now, at last, you can turn to educational psychology itself in the form of Stones' *Introduction to Educational Psychology*. If you have done your course of reading, you will get much more out of Stones than if you had started with a book like this. You can go on to Lovell's *Educational Psychology and Children*, Butcher's *Human Intelligence* or Stones' anthology *Readings in Educational Psychology*.

Finally, if your appetite is really whetted and you find yourself consuming psychology paperbacks as if they were thrillers, attempt the psychological equivalent of *War and Peace* by reading William James' *Principles of Psychology*, eighty years old and almost as fresh as when it was written.

Books mentioned

Abercrombie, M. L. J., *The Anatomy of Judgement*, Penguin, 1969.
Adcock, C. J., *Fundamentals of Psychology*, Penguin, 1964.
Arnheim, R., *Visual Thinking*, Faber & Faber, 1970.
Barnett, S. A., *Instinct and Intelligence*, Penguin, 1970.
Boyle, D. G., *Student's Guide to Piaget*, Pergamon, 1969.
Bruner, J. S., *The Process of Education*, New York: Vintage Books, 1960.
Bruner, J. S., **Goodnow**, J. J. and **Austin**, G. A., *A Study of Thinking*, New York: Wiley, 1956.
Butcher, H. J., *Human Intelligence*, Methuen: University Paperbacks, 1970.
Cattell, R. B., *The Scientific Analysis of Personality*, Penguin, 1965.
Clark, D. Stafford, *What Freud Really Said*, Penguin, 1967.
Gagné, R. M., *The Conditions of Learning*, New York: Holt, Rinehart & Winston, 1965.
Gesell, A. and **Ilg**, F. L., *Child Development*, two vols, New York: Harper, 1946.
Gesell, A., **Ilg**, F. L., and **Ames**, L. B., *Youth: the Years from Ten to Sixteen*, New York: Harper, 1956.
Gregory, R. L., *Eye and Brain*, Weidenfeld & Nicolson, 1966.
Hebb, D. O., *The Organization of Behaviour*, New York: Wiley, 1949.
Hebb, D. O., *A Textbook of Psychology*, Saunders, 2nd ed. 1966.
Hudson, L., *Contrary Imaginations*, Penguin, 1966.
James, W., *The Principles of Psychology*, Macmillan, 1890.
Jones, E., *Life and Work of Sigmund Freud*, Penguin, 1967.
Kohler, W., *The Mentality of Apes*, New York: 1931.
Lovell, K., *Educational Psychology and Children*, University of London, 1969 edition.
Luria, A. S., *The Mind of the Mnemonist*, Cape, 1969.

McKellar, P., *Experience and Behaviour*, Penguin, 1968.
Sprott, W. H. J., *Human Groups*, Penguin, 1958.
Stones, E., *Introduction to Educational Psychology*, Methuen: University Paperbacks, 1966.
Stones, E., *Readings in Educational Psychology*, Methuen: University Paperbacks, 1970.
Thurber, J., *Let Your Mind Alone*, Hamish Hamilton, 1937.
Valentine, C. W., *The Normal Child and Some of his Abnormalities*, Penguin, 1956.
Walter, W. Grey, *The Living Brain*, Duckworth, 1953.
Wright, D. S., et al., *Introducing Psychology: an Experimental Approach*, Penguin, 1970.

3

The Sociology of Education

Anne Dufton

Although a relatively recent development, the study of sociology of education has by now achieved tremendous importance and takes its place alongside psychology, philosophy and history as one of the principal elements in the education course. This is not to suggest that education can be divided neatly up into separate compartments (though unfortunately it is often taught as if it could be). The sociologist, psychologist, historian and philosopher each approach the study of education from their specialist disciplines, and in this chapter I hope to show how the sociologist brings his particular skills to bear. The reader should then attempt to place this in the context of the historical, philosophical and psychological perspective described in other chapters of this book.

Then again, the sociology of education is just one aspect of the discipline of sociology. So we must begin by looking at sociology as a whole before attempting to define one of its constituent elements. In broad terms, the sociologist is concerned with man in society, his behaviour, his ideas and institutions (Marsh, 1965; Cotgrove, 1967). Within this framework the sociologist is inevitably concerned with the institution of education, with its relationship with the economy and social mobility and with the relationship between education and social change. More detailed analysis may be concerned with the school system and with the organization of particular schools; it may consider teaching as a profession and the relationship between teachers and pupils; and it may attempt to define the role of the school in that complex process whereby values and attitudes are acquired.

It is not the aim of a sociology of education course to train sophisticated sociologists who can undertake this kind of detailed analysis but rather to enable the intending teacher to examine the major issues in society (which are so often the major issues in education) using some of the techniques and skills of the sociologist. It is not sufficient, as some would seem to suggest, merely to develop a critical awareness, a questioning attitude. Such a course must also show how sociology seeks answers, sifts evidence, discriminates between fact and opinion; without attempting to produce experts it must provide an informed understanding of the methods and techniques of social investigation and statistical analysis. Such a programme of work will develop the skills which are necessary to interpret the growing body of educational research (so much of which has employed psychology and sociology in its methodology), and, equally, it will develop the skills of evaluation required by teachers when examining their own work in the school and when faced with new ideas about teaching methods, school organization and patterns of relationship. Professor William Taylor expresses this concisely:

> The justification for the inclusion of sociological studies in the course for intending teachers does not rest upon any observable link between the pursuit of such studies and the improvement of classroom techniques and practice. Rather it is dependent upon the requirement that the teacher should first of all be capable of thinking logically and rationally about the whole range of social phenomena that he encounters in his personal and professional life. It is this rational intellect, the ability to sort out fact and value judgement, the respect for evidence, the capacity for making generalisations (Taylor, 1966).

Professor Taylor makes the important point that the sociology of education course is concerned to develop this awareness in the individual as an individual, not merely as a student teacher.

It is clearly not possible within the confines of a single chapter to illustrate the whole range of the sociology of education, and indeed courses in the different colleges at present vary quite considerably (see p. 60). At the end of this section there is a summary of the kinds of topic generally included in a sociology of education course, but a more detailed description will first be given of one particular sociological concept, showing how it can be used to analyse a variety of situations within the education system. The one chosen is that of 'role', because it illustrates many situations with which the reader is already familiar.

The concept of role

The sociologist can look at society in a number of ways. One way sees society as a social system, a system in which individuals or groups of people are involved in patterns of relationships. Many of these relationships are clearly defined, as, for example, that between a doctor and his patient. Others which were once clearly defined have been undergoing change, as between employer and employee, teacher and pupil. This may lead to some uncertainty for both parties in the relationship. Confusion and uncertainty can arise if the pattern of behaviour which ought to be followed is not very clear.

The sociologist refers to these relationships as roles: there is the employer role and the employee role, the teacher role and the pupil role. Usually we are prepared for these different roles from an early age and come to accept the general order of relationships in society, but we never have just one role. The pupil is at the same time boy or girl, son or daughter, elder son or elder daughter, soccer fan, amateur photographer, folk singer and so on. All these facets interact in the one person. Occasionally they may conflict, as when one's responsibilities as son or daughter are at variance with one's enthusiasm for soccer, or when the school's expectations of pupil conformity conflicts with the pupil's own perception of himself as an adult with the right to determine his own choice of say length of hair (boys) or of skirt (girls).

The last point illustrates the fact that role is a two-way concept, that is, any role involves the values and expectations of the individual as he sees them himself and as they are seen by others, what is often called the self-image and the public-image. Thus the teacher believes that he must act in a certain way and the pupil expects the teacher to behave in a certain way. To a certain extent, then, their behaviour is predictable, and this makes it easier for both pupil and teacher to interact, easier than if every time the two came into contact with each other they were to behave in vastly different ways.

The process whereby the individual teacher acquires this perception of his role is a very complex one. It includes his own experiences of teachers when he was a pupil – teachers who were admired and teachers who were detested – and pleasant and unpleasant memories of school life. This together with the kind of training received and early teaching experiences will determine the individual teacher's view of his role. But there is more than one set of expectations. Not only does the pupil expect the teacher to behave in a certain way, so also do parents, school inspectors, headteachers and so on. And indeed the teacher may interpret his role rather differently according to whom he is with and moderate his behaviour accordingly. Occasionally people from the different groups may come together and the teacher is faced with the dilemma of his different behaviour patterns. For example, a teacher who maintains a rigid, authoritarian regime when in the classroom is holidaying with his family; during horseplay with his youngsters on the beach he is conscious of a group of pupils from his class observing his highly uncharacteristic behaviour with some obvious amusement. Does he ignore his pupils and continue acting the fool? Does he, to the surprise of his own youngsters, immediately become stiff and formal? Does he draw his pupils into the game and risk a loss of authority after the holidays when school re-opens? And are there any other courses of action which he could take?

This idea of the teacher playing a very definite role which is maintained in the classroom and in private life is illustrated clearly in this quotation from what is now regarded as a classic study of teachers:

> According to the teacher code there is no worse offence than failure to deport one's self with dignity, and the penalties exacted for the infraction of the code are severe (Waller, 1965).

Waller was, of course, writing in 1932 and was writing about the American teacher, but this passage does demonstrate what we would regard today as very severe expectations of the community for its teachers. This picture has changed and is changing, but there are still occasions when the individual may face a conflict between his teacher life and his private life (as illustrated by the teacher on holiday). This last situation is usually referred to as role conflict, and another example may illustrate it further.

In recent teacher-strikes, many felt a conflict of loyalties. Their concern for the welfare of the children they taught was in conflict with their concern for their own professional standing as expressed by their unions. To strike was to express the solidarity of the profession and bring pressure to bear on the employers for better wages and working conditions which would ultimately be to the benefit of the pupils. But to strike was inevitably to their short-term disadvantage.

Obviously there is a good deal more in the concept of role than this: for a more detailed description, a good introductory book is M. Banton, *Roles: An Introduction to the Study of Social Relations* (1965).

We shall now move on to use this concept to analyse in simple terms the role of the school, the teacher, the parent, the pupil, ancillary services and finally that of education in society.

The role of the school

The school is an agent of socialization. Socialization is an important concept in education: it is the process whereby the individual acquires the values and attitudes which are a mark of his individual personality. The process begins in the cradle when his mother either ignores the crying baby or constantly picks it up; it continues through childhood when concepts of right and wrong are developed according to parental expectations. Indeed, research has increasingly shown that it is family experiences in early childhood which are most important in shaping the future adult, but there are other agencies involved in this process, notably schools, the mass media and, for some, organized religion.

The relative importance of these other agencies of socialization varies according to individual circumstances for each child, but whatever his background, whether he is born into a loving or a rejecting family circle, whether he is illegitimate or orphaned, whether he is highly endowed with intellectual ability or mentally retarded, schooling is compulsory. The school therefore is (or can be) the most important agent of socialization after the family. The reasons for this predominance are many. The school offers the key to intellectual advancement and personal achievement; the school interprets and re-inforces the values of society. But this is a complicated process because the early years in the family are such vital ones and because the child in the school reflects in his behaviour, attitudes and aspirations, the attitudes and aspirations of his home. Some children, for example, come from more privileged backgrounds where education is seen as desirable and all important; others come from homes where schooling is seen as a necessary evil. The school must therefore have not one but a variety of keys, almost as many as it has pupils, to try and ensure that each individual child has an opportunity for intellectual and personal development. So to speak of the school as *the* key is misleading, and indeed the erroneous belief that equal educational provision ensures equal educational opportunity is at the root of much educational deprivation (Plowden Report, 1967).

An understanding of the process of socialization is therefore an essential aspect of the study of the role of the school. But it is always difficult to interpret a process in which we ourselves are

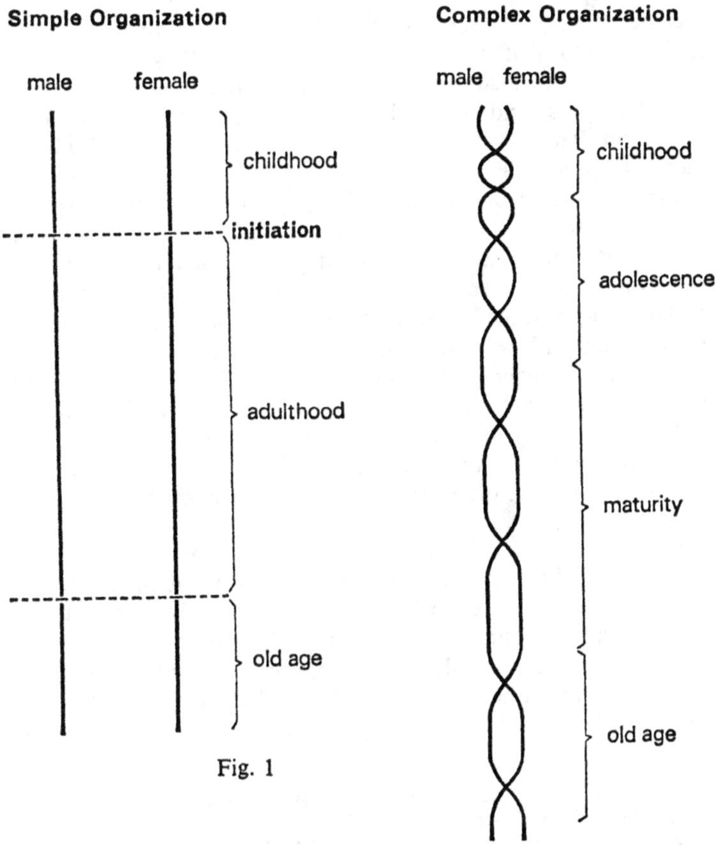

Simple Organization — male, female: childhood, initiation, adulthood, old age

Complex Organization — male, female: childhood, adolescence, maturity, old age

Fig. 1

closely involved, and we are all involved in education, whether as pupils in school, students in college, teachers, tutors, parents or taxpayers. Sociologists working within a complex and rapidly changing society such as ours often face this difficulty of disentangling the many interweaving, interlocking strands which make up a social situation. Theoretical models have been developed to assist the sociologist in this process. It can also be helpful to turn to the analysis of a less complex society provided by anthropology, for such an analysis may help us to clarify further the process of socialization.

The much simplified diagram in Figure 1 illustrates this process in the simple organization found in some African and Pacific societies, before the societies themselves became involved in the rapid evolution of our technological age. In the simple society children are socialized from birth into their appropriate roles as boys and girls, and their education is the responsibility of the male and female members of the society. Even in childhood there is often a demarcation between boys and girls, the boys spending more time with the adult men, the girls with the women. At a definite time, usually referred to as initiation, childhood ceases, and the occasion is marked by religious and ceremonial observances which vary from one culture to another in length and intensity and the age at which they take place. At this time, the young man will be told about his future responsibilities as an adult male member of the society, he will be inducted into the religious sects of the adult men, he will be told of his rights and obligations. The young woman will be similarly instructed in her role. As new adults they will play their full part in society, and they will note that other adults in the society respect their rights and obligations.

In the diagram of the contemporary society we can see that the period of childhood and adulthood merge through a period of adolescence, there are no known and universally accepted times when a child becomes a young person and the young person becomes an adult. Similarly, the role of male and female are no longer clearly delineated, and, increasingly, exactly similar education, work and leisure are open equally to both male and female.*

* As an interesting and informative exercise, draw up a list of the ways in which the male and female roles still differ, and attempt to predict any future changes and the role of education in that process.

Unlike those in the simple society, modern laws can be seen to be interpreted in different ways by different groups, and the society as a whole does not necessarily agree on what is right, just, good, etc. Further, the adults may extol one set of values and behaviour patterns as essential to the preservation of social order, but be seen to behave themselves in a different way. This can be confusing for young people at a time when they are seeking personal and social identity. Thus it is that the child in contemporary society may find at school that teachers have a different pattern of expectations from that which is prevalent in his own family and home neighbourhood. For example, the home may be a place where lying, swearing, cheating are commonplace. A child acting in the same way in the home may get a cuff on the ear but is not seriously deterred from copying his elders. In the school, he finds that this behaviour is frowned upon and punished. In this kind of situation the school may provide a source of conflict for the child rather than act as a vehicle of achievement. Another example is of the pupil who does well in school and is encouraged to pursue his studies beyond the school leaving age. His parents, however, see little value in education beyond the minimum requirement and press him to leave school and get a job with good pay and prospects. In a situation in which school and home lack easy communication, the child is pulled one way and the other between conflicting advice and pressures. This can be shown diagrammatically (Fig. 2). In diagram A, the aims, expectations, aspirations, etc. of the home and the school are in reasonable accord; there is harmony between teachers and parents and the interflow of relationships enables the child to achieve his

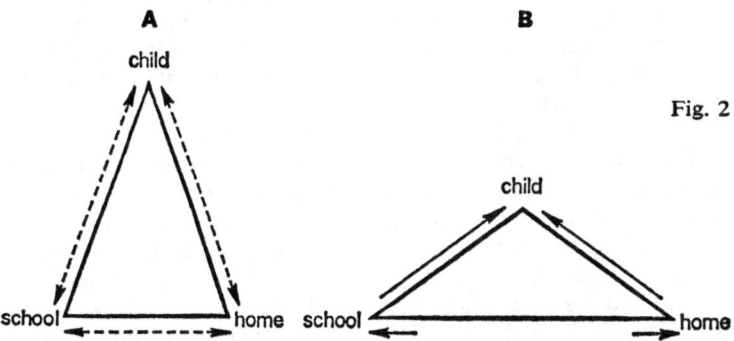

Fig. 2

individual performance peak. In B, the situation is more complex; the attitudes of parents and teachers are far apart, the line of communication between home and school is broken and conflicting demands are being made upon the child. This acts as a pressure and a source of conflict and limits the progress of the child so that he may be underachieving.

It is for this reason that the teacher in training is asked to study the different kinds of culture groups (sub-cultures) and to consider the role of the school as an agency of socialization particularly in those sub-cultures where school and home can be (at least potentially) in conflict (Mays, 1962). Such study will involve analysis of family structures, beliefs, aspirations, attitudes and values. It will consider aspects of social, cultural and emotional deprivation, such as living in overcrowded accommodation (Douglas, 1964), the particular difficulties of children from broken homes (Kellmer-Pringle et al., 1966) and the needs of children from families where the educational aspirations of parents for their children may be limited for a variety of reasons (Jackson and Marsden, 1962) or where educational aspiration is high but the pre-school experiences of children have been limited because parents have not understood the importance of play experience and particularly of early language development through conversation with adults (Bereiter and Englemann, 1966; Bernstein, 1967).

The role of the teacher

The school does not exist without the teachers and pupils who constitute it, and the increasing number of studies of the teacher reflect his changing role as the education system itself is changing. When using the concept of role to analyse the work of the teacher, it is important to remember that the person who is a teacher is many other things as well. The teacher may be a wife or husband, mother or father, amateur actor, keen collector of antiques, poet, playwright, badminton champion and so on. All these roles make up the one person, and though any one may be predominant at a particular time, they all interact. Thus the man who is both teacher and amateur actor may use his skills to help in his approach to the teaching of English, but when he is performing his role as teacher, his role as teacher is the one which is paramount and that as amateur actor incidental. In each of these roles we may have quite different behaviour patterns or speech patterns.

Consider for example one's behaviour and speech with a group in the school playground and one's behaviour and speech when in the classroom or addressing the headteacher.

In this section, we concentrate on the different kinds of teacher roles found in the school. Any study of the role of the teacher will differentiate between assistant teacher and headteacher, between primary school teacher and secondary school teacher, between male and female teacher. These distinctions are concerned not only with the different work that is done but with the more subtle but tremendously important differing attitudes and expectations of the individuals concerned (role incumbents). For example, for a long time the infant school teacher was associated with a mother role and infant school teaching was therefore thought to be far more suitable for women; the work was regarded as at an elementary level and therefore more suitable for the less academic woman. Junior schools were seen as rather more demanding but still not requiring a very high level of academic ability. Smaller sized units with fewer career prospects than the secondary school, they were also mainly the preserve of the woman teacher. Secondary schools, on the other hand, provided opportunities for specializing in one or two subjects and required more academic qualifications. There were more opportunities for promotions and for graded posts, and salary scales were higher; these opportunities attracted more men. The grammar schools were seen as catering for the intellectual cream and attracted the graduate teachers (Tropp, 1957). (An interesting analysis of some of the effects of the concentration of women in primary education is given in Brookover, *A Sociology of Education*, 1955.)

Thus a hierarchy was established with infant teachers at the bottom and grammar school teachers at the top. This image has tended to remain despite increasing evidence to show that early concept formation is the basis of later intellectual development or, put another way, that unless the child in the infant school receives expert teaching, the junior school may be unable to compensate and the secondary school will certainly be too late. This is not to suggest that the hierarchy should be stood on its head, but rather that we should recognize each role as equally demanding and rewarding within its own sphere of operation. This hierarchy was not only seen by teachers but also by parents, and the status which accrued to grammar schools and public schools still remains. The proposed legislation of the 1970 government to impose a comprehensive secondary education system and the arguments put forward against such legislation provide a fascinating study. It is therefore important that those who are professionally engaged in education (and this includes teachers and administrators) should understand the factors which influence decisions about educational organization.

In the same way that we detect a hierarchy between schools, we can also recognize a hierarchy within schools. The most obvious is that which exists between assistant teachers, heads of department, the deputy head and the head. In British schools the headteacher has traditionally been the architect of school policy; under his leadership the school aquires its distinctive characteristics, its emphasis on examination success, community service, sports predominance and so on. Usually the headteacher will tend to gather around him a staff which supports his ideals. Thus within the school a teacher may face role conflict (see p. 47) when his ideals of his role are contrary to those held by his headteacher. Some who disagree may simply appear to conform, others may carry on in permanent conflict, yet others may seek posts in other schools. More subtle, but of real importance, is the distinction which can be found in many secondary schools between the specialist subject teacher and the general subjects teacher (Shipman, 1968), between the graduate and the non-graduate (Cannon, 1964), and these distinctions are made by both staff and pupils. Such understanding enables teachers to appraise and evaluate their own position and can also contribute to an acceptance of new approaches in education. For example, it is sometimes difficult for teachers who see themselves as specialist teachers in a particular subject to accept an approach which is based upon contributions from a team of teachers to a general course such as 'Man in Society' (Hoyle, 1969; Morrison and McIntyre, 1969).

Many attempts have been made to define the role of the teacher in the school. Such definitions refer to the instructional role – inculcation of knowledge, development of skills – the pastoral role – care and concern for young people with particular difficulties which may arise from home circumstances – the socializing role – concerned with the inculcation of values, 'right' kinds of attitudes, preparation for future life in society and so on.

It is sometimes suggested that teachers may give priority to one or another of these aspects of their work. One teacher, for example, gives more weight to instruction, another lays emphasis on socialization and yet another devotes most time and effort to the welfare needs of his pupils. It is probably true that the vast majority of teachers find it easier to define the part they play in instruction than the part they play in socialization. It is not my purpose here to consider whether or not any one of these three aspects of teaching is more important than another or is seen by teachers or parents to be more important, but a useful analysis can be found in Musgrove and Taylor (1969).

Finally, in this section on the teacher it is essential to consider a new kind of specialization which is emerging in both primary and secondary schools. These specialists are particularly concerned with the welfare and guidance of pupils and are variously called 'teacher–social workers', 'teacher–counsellors', 'counsellors' or 'home liaison officers', and there are many other names. Their work is an extension of the pastoral role referred to above, but this development does not necessarily lessen the need for all teachers to be concerned with the welfare of the pupils whom they teach – their concern and involvement continues. However, not all teachers are agreed that such specialist appointments are a good thing. The sociologist is interested in these differing attitudes, in the way in which these specialist roles are developing in different schools and in whether there is any conflict for the person who is both teacher (often stereotyped as being authoritarian) and counsellor (often stereotyped as permissive). Similarly, there is interest in whether pupils find any difficulty in confiding in the specialist who is a member of the staff of the school, which may represent a place of continual failure and impossible demands in respect of discipline and loyalty. On a wider plane, the sociologist is concerned with the suggestion that provision of guidance and counselling services within the education system is allowing the family (particularly parents) to opt out of this part of its function. Study of these factors at the training stage may help the teacher to understand his own position in relation to new specialist roles in the school, and it may go some way towards breaking down the barriers which sometimes exist in schools which offer a counselling service.

The role of the pupil

Any study of the role of the school cannot be divorced from a study of the role of the pupil. Historical analysis will show that education for boys and girls was initially conceived in different terms, as was education of the children of the rich and the poor. The pupil in the Board School was taught, along with the three Rs and moral rectitude, that the teacher was always right; lessons based on rote learning did not encourage questioning. The girl was seen as a future wife and mother who need not be too concerned with matters other than domestic. The boy was schooled into his future position as breadwinner.

In contrast, the pupil today is often encouraged to discover in the humanities, to seek causes in science and to find relationships in mathematics. This approach is altering his relationship with his instructors from that of the teacher and the taught to that of partners in learning, and although the teacher is, as it were, master planner, the pupils are themselves engaged in developing the curriculum. Such an approach makes very real demands upon the teacher, and therefore a thorough understanding of the process is essential if the necessary adjustments are to be made. Another example of the changing relationship is to be found in school councils, which consist of representatives of staff and pupils and may include discipline committees. (A more recent example is the development of so-called 'pupil power'.)

Within schools there may be a hierarchy of pupils. For example, in the junior school, status will accrue to pupils who make the staff tea or wash the cups and saucers; in the secondary school to class prefects and house prefects. But it is essential to distinguish between the formal status which is gained from an official appointment, such as prefect, and the informal status which may be acquired by individuals or groups within their own age band (peer group). Reference was made in the section on socialization to the importance of the family; similar emphasis should be placed on the influence of the peer group. The importance of the peer group may be best described by noting the way in which a young person with reasonably neutral attitudes to school, placed in a group which has high educational aspiration, will be drawn along by the general urgency to complete homework, achieve good marks and please the teacher. The same youngster in a group which is apathetic or hostile to academic success will be drawn along by the general disregard for completing homework or achieving good marks and will seek to make school bearable by teacher-baiting. Sometimes schools unintentionally re-inforce

tional welfare, school health, child care, probation and voluntary social welfare agencies. These services provide specialists who work with children and families with special needs: they work with the delinquent and the maladjusted, with the feckless and the sick. Along with the teacher, they are members of the caring professions, that is, their concern is with the individual and the family in the community, and their aim is to help the individual to come to an awareness of his problem and to increase his capacity to deal with it by providing a co-operative relationship and by bringing the skills of the profession to bear upon it (Hancock and Willmott, 1965).

The teacher in training will therefore study the work of these professions for three reasons:

a. to gain an insight into the work of different professional groups as it has a bearing upon the needs of children and their families. In this way, it may be easier to achieve essential co-operation between these related professions.
b. to have appropriate knowledge of specialist agencies to enable referral of children with special needs.
c. to compare the approaches and methods of different specialist professional groups and to consider whether, for example, the role of teacher and the role of social worker are necessarily different.

The teacher can no longer work in isolation bounded by the four walls of the classroom. The mass of evidence pointing to the influence of the home and the sub-culture on educational achievement, to which reference has been made throughout this section on the concept of role, underlines the importance of co-operation between education and all the social services. (For a further treatment of this point see Birley and Dufton, 1971.)

The role of education in society

Finally, no study of role in the context of education would be complete without reference to the role of education in society. At this point the different disciplines in the study of education are brought together, for an understanding of education in society requires a historical, philosophical, psychological and sociological perspective. Three examples of the kind of questions asked are:

a. Is the process of social change shaped by the educational

system or does the educational system alter in response to a changing society?
b. To what extent does the school curriculum reflect the specialist needs of society?
c. How far does or should education attempt to shape values and attitudes in young people?

There is probably no finite answer to questions such as these which are concerned with goals in education. But for the teacher in training, the questions raised in a study of the sociology of education are vital ones, for even the very new teacher working in the reception class in the infant school is consciously or unwittingly an agent of social change.

The sociology of education course

This glimpse into the concept of role as applied to education has necessarily been brief and superficial, but I hope that it has helped to illustrate one of the ways in which the sociologist looks at education. It is doubtful if any sociology of education course would be developed solely from a study of role, and therefore the remainder of this chapter is devoted to a brief analysis of the major elements.

In the college of education it is probable that sociology of education will be studied as an integral element in the education course. Colleges vary in their organization, and it may be taught in one year or spread over the three years of the course. Similarly, there is considerable variation in the weighting of time which is given to the sociological aspects of education. Those colleges which offer a B.Ed. degree generally allow an element of specialization in the fourth year, and this might include options in some aspect of educational sociology. In the one-year post-graduate course, the time available is obviously more limited and the extent to which sociology can be studied in depth will be restricted. A recent development is a special course with emphasis on social work for graduates in the social sciences* which can assume a more sophisticated knowledge of sociology. The social work aspects involve an application of the principles of social work training to teaching with as many opportunities as possible for practical field work experience. The course considers the kind of points raised on p. 59.

*This course is run by the Education Department in co-operation with the Social Sciences Department of Edge Hill College of Education, Ormskirk.

The study of sociology of education does not aim to produce a sophisticated knowledge of sociology, for this just would not be possible in the time available. But it is essential to include a grounding in general sociological theory to provide a sound theoretical framework within which empirical discussion can take place. Ways of approaching this introductory section can vary considerably but it would normally include a brief review of the development of sociology and an examination of some of its basic concepts (as, for example, role), and an important section would be the examination of techniques of social investigation and statistical methods.

In this section it would also be necessary to define the terms of reference within which the study of education would take place.

The main part of the course includes topics such as:

Socialization:
- the family
- social class
- values and attitudes
- the material environment
- the peer group
- mass media

Educational opportunity:
- linguistic development
- social factors in learning
- occupational choices

The schools:
- their structure and function
- the role of the teacher
- the role of the pupil
- the school and the community
- organization, at local and central levels

Social psychology:
- the study of groups
- sociometry
- authority and leadership

Social pathology:
- social problems in education
- delinquency and crime
- deviance

62 *Anne Dufton*

Social structure: the family, marriage and divorce
social class
mobility
the social services
urbanization

Education and social
 change: values, norms, ideologies, goals
democracy
economic development

But nearly all these topics are interrelated. Thus Figure 3 shows that if the child is taken as the starting point, it is necessary to consider the socialization process which he undergoes in his family and home neighbourhood. Then there are the influences brought to bear by the mass media in society. His social class is initially determined by his family, but the school provides an opportunity through education to achieve a higher

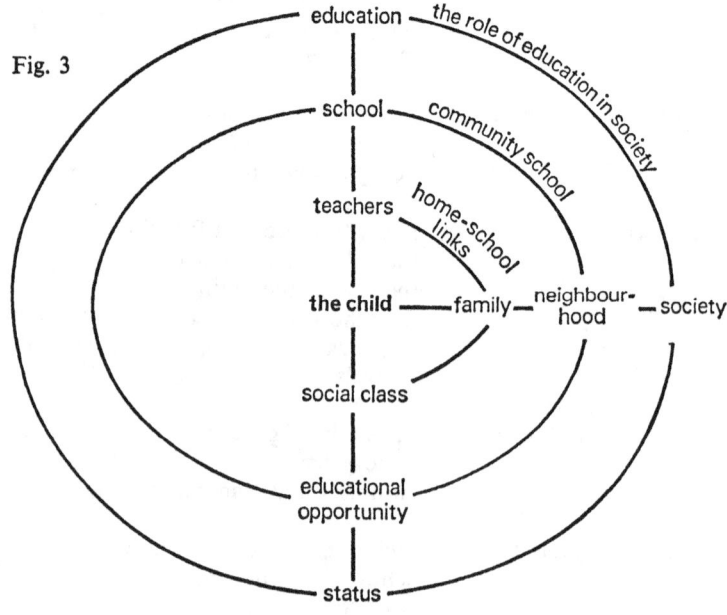

Fig. 3

status (determined largely by social factors) than his parents'. For those children who start at a disadvantage, strong links are required between teachers and parents, school and neighbourhood, if the value of education is to be recognized, and all this must be seen in the context of the role of education in society.

A final quotation from Susanne Langer illustrates the interrelatedness of all the disciplines concerned with the study of education:

To determine the aims of education is probably the most urgent philosophical problem in the whole pedagogical field today; and it cannot but draw in further vast questions of the aims of human societies, the ultimate values that set up these aims, our basic ideals of society and individual life. Seriously pursued it may lead to entirely new definitions of 'society', 'life', 'individual', 'purpose', 'action', and other terms, to some unpredictable number and perhaps in startling ways – until we find ourselves in a new formulation of our whole modern 'weltanschauung', which is vague and dark at present, in this stormy age of transition to some new world that no one can yet foresee (Langer, 1956).

References and further reading

Banton, M., *Roles: An Introduction to the Study of Social Relations*, Tavistock, 1965.
Bereiter, C., and Englemann, S., *Teaching Disadvantaged Children in the Pre-School*, New York: Prentice Hall, 1966.
Bernstein, B., 'Social Structure, Language and Learning' in M. Craft, J. Rayner, and L. Cohen, eds, *Linking Home and School*, Longmans Green, 1967.
Birley, D., and Dufton, A., *An Equal Chance*, Routledge & Kegan Paul, 1971.
Brookover, W. B., *A Sociology of Education*, New York: American Book Company, 1955.
Cannon, C., 'Some Variations on the Teacher's Role', *Education for Teaching*, May 1964.
Cotgrove, S., *The Science of Society*, Allen & Unwin, 1967.
Douglas, J. W. B., *The Home and the School*, MacGibbon & Kee, 1964.
Evans, K. M., *Sociometry and Education*, Routledge & Kegan Paul, 1962.
Hancock, A., and Willmott, P., *The Social Workers*, British Broadcasting Corporation, 1965.
Hargreaves, D. H., *Social Relations in the Secondary School*, Routledge & Kegan Paul, 1967.
Horton, P. B., and Hunt, B. L., *Sociology*, New York: McGraw Hill Book Company, 1964.

Hoyle, E., *The Role of the Teacher*, Routledge & Kegan Paul, 1969.
Jackson, B., and Marsden, D., *Education and the Working Class*, Routledge & Kegan Paul, 1962.
Kellmer-Pringle, M., Butler, N. R., Davie, R., *1100 Seven Year Olds*, Longmans Green, 1966.
Langer, S., 'On the Relations between Philosophy and Education', *Harvard Educational Review*, 26 (Spring 1956), pp. 139–41.
Marsh, D. C., *The Social Sciences*, Routledge & Kegan Paul, 1965.
Mays, J. B., *Education and the Urban Child*, Liverpool University Press, 1962.
Morrison, A., and McIntyre, D., *Teachers and Teaching*, Penguin, 1969.
Musgrove, F., and Taylor, P. H., *Society and the Teacher's Role*, Routledge & Kegan Paul, 1969.
Plowden Report, *Children and their Primary Schools*, Report of the Central Advisory Council on Education (England), H.M.S.O., 1967.
Riley, M. W., *Sociological Research, A Case Approach*, New York: Harcourt, Brace & World, 1963.
Rosenthal, R. H., and Jacobson, L., *Pygmalion in the Classroom*, New York: Holt, Rinehart & Winston, 1968.
Shipman, M., *Sociology of the School*, Longmans Green, 1968.
Taylor, W., *The Study of Education*, Routledge & Kegan Paul, 1966, p. 210.
Tropp, A., *The School Teachers*, Heinemann, 1957.
Waller, W., *The Sociology of Teaching*, New York: Wiley, Science Editions, 1965, p. 389.
Webb, J., 'The Sociology of the School', *British Journal of Sociology*, viii, 3 (1962), pp. 264–72.

4

The History of Education
Malcolm Seaborne

The first university professorships in education, established at Edinburgh and St Andrews in the 1870s, were in the 'Theory, History and Practice of Education', and, as earlier chapters in this book have shown, history, along with psychology, was among the first of the special disciplines which were applied to education as an academic study.[1] This was at a time when the study of history generally was expanding in institutions of higher education and when much of the effort of professional historians was directed towards the elucidation of the political and constitutional aspects of the subject. Training colleges for intending teachers had been set up after about 1840, and, towards the end of the nineteenth century, the study of the history of education spread into these colleges, where the emphasis, as in the universities of the time, was placed on the development of institutions and particularly on the part which the central government played in educational policy following the setting up of the Committee of Council on Education in 1839 and including, of course, the introduction of universal compulsory education following the Education Act of 1870.

Two basic difficulties, however, arose in connection with the study of the history of education in training colleges and later in the university departments of education which were established in 1911. The first was common to the other branches of education discussed in this book, viz. the lack of specialization among the lecturing staff, which often resulted in entrusting the historical aspect to lecturers who were experienced schoolteachers, but were rarely acquainted with the more general developments in historical teaching and research. The second difficulty, though arising from the first, was peculiar to the history of education. As we have already seen, the study of this branch of education began towards the end of the nineteenth century when the constitutional aspects of history were considered to be all-important, illustrating as they did the triumph of parliamentary democracy in Britain. Unfortunately, this tendency to concentrate on the history of institutions remained dominant in the colleges and departments of education although, as we shall see, the history faculties in the universities of the twentieth century soon began to broaden the subject beyond the purely constitutional and political aspects. In the colleges and departments, however, courses in what have been aptly dubbed 'Acts and Facts' continued to be inflicted on generations of students and tended to give the history of education a bad name.

Now anyone acquainted with the development of historical studies outside the colleges and departments of education will know that the earlier concentration on purely constitutional history has largely disappeared, and, though the study of institutions continues to play an important part in most undergraduate courses in history, this study has itself been broadened out to show how the development of institutions has reflected many aspects of national life. In addition, the economic depression of the inter-war period and the series of diplomatic crises which eventually led to the outbreak of the Second World War resulted in a shift of interest towards economic and international history. Yet in the colleges the economic and comparative aspects of educational history were still almost wholly neglected. In more recent years, further major changes have taken place in the study of history generally. The development of welfare policies by both central and local government authorities has reflected a renewed interest in the lives of ordinary people, rather than in the exploits of rulers and politicians (though there is always likely to be a certain fascination in reading about the outstanding personalities of any period). This interest in the doings of the mass of the people has also been closely related to the emergence of sociology which, though it remains a separate discipline, has interacted at many points with historical studies. Another notable post-war phenomenon has been the way in which history has been studied in relation to many other aspects of human endeavour: thus, it is now much more usual to consider the literary, artistic and scientific achievements of the past and also to pay a great deal more attention to local history with its many ramifications. Some historians, indeed, have suggested that history has a unique role to play in bringing together an unusually large number of branches of the study of human society.

In many secondary schools in the 1940s and 1950s, the study of political and diplomatic history at the Ordinary and Advanced levels of the G.C.E. was still the order of the day. Just as in the colleges and departments of education, there has been a considerable time lag between the introduction of new historical studies into the universities and their introduction, in simplified (and, alas, also sometimes distorted) form into the schools. But in the 1960s the schools gave more attention to social and economic history, and other ways of looking at history were beginning to be explored, particularly at C.S.E. level and in the general courses given in some sixth forms. The appearance of 'archive teaching units' in the schools also gave at least some pupils the opportunity to appreciate for themselves the nature of the original sources upon which the generalizations of the textbooks are based.[2]

How far are the changes in the content and method of studying history in the universities and, to a lesser extent, in the schools, also being reflected in the courses now being given to students at colleges and departments of education? Do we find that the colleges have acted as pace-makers or have they, like so many schools, followed in the wake of new educational developments? Unfortunately (though a thorough historical as well as contemporary examination of this question would be needed to answer it with any degree of accuracy) it is probably the case that the latter rather than the former represents the truer general picture. A survey of courses on the history of education was carried out in 1967 and showed that the new approaches described above were beginning to make an impact, but that, at least in some colleges and departments, the general despair which the study of 'Acts and Facts' produced had led to the abandonment of any specifically historical component in the education course.[3] It was because of the need for a radical rethinking of such courses that, also in 1967, a History of Education Society was formed by lecturers in colleges and departments of education to organize conferences and issue bulletins giving publicity to the more interesting new developments which were beginning to take place. It is also now becoming more usual to employ specialist historians to give courses on the history of education, and there is growing evidence of a marked revival of interest in this aspect of education.

There has never been any serious doubt that the historical aspect of education must be studied if the developments of the present day are to be seen in perspective and understood at more than a purely superficial level. The problem is how to make such a study relevant and palatable to students who may have dropped history several years ago or suffered from bad teaching of the subject earlier in their school careers. A further general point needs to be considered concerning this question of relevance, though again it applies not only to the particular branch of historical study which we call the history of education, but to the study of history as a whole. This is the theoretical point made by some recent philosophical writers, who suggest that the essential value of history lies in the experience which it gives of handling particular sorts of evidence and in re-creating imaginatively situations very different from our own. Such a study, it is maintained, is justifiable in its own right, and a predominant concern with practical present-day problems may prevent one from entering fully into the past.[4] Other writers, of more 'artistic' temperament, stress the inherent fascination of the past and see history purely as an interesting intellectual pursuit.

Though curiosity about the past, and especially about unusual people in history, is extremely widespread (think of all the novels and films with a semi-historical background) the kind of arguments mentioned above are not strong enough to ensure the place of history in schools and colleges, especially if a claim is advanced that every child and student should study it, since, apart from anything else, some individuals are simply bored by the kind of history dispensed at many institutions. The question of relevance, not necessarily to the immediate present but to the particular stage of education which a student has reached, is therefore very important and is raised in an acute form when it comes to selecting the period or periods of history to study in some depth. There has recently been a marked tendency in the schools, and perhaps to a lesser extent in the universities, to study 'contemporary history', in spite of the criticisms commonly made that objectivity (which in history is anyhow a relative term) is impossible to attain, quite apart from other difficulties such as the sheer mass of evidence available for study.⁵ The more traditional view is that in a sense no one period is more or less profitable to study than another, since practice in handling historical evidence and making historical judgments (which are the stock-in-trade of the historian) can equally well be given in any period – indeed, some would argue that the more distant the period the better, since the evidence can then be sifted more carefully and the imaginative leap required is greater for periods remote in time. This line of thought, however, has come up against opposition from many teachers and students who feel very strongly that the study of the past must be of more direct use in helping to solve some of the many problems which beset us in the modern world.

These apparently theoretical arguments should not be dismissed as unimportant, as they sometimes are by professional historians. Certainly, so far as the study of education is concerned, one of the besetting weaknesses in the past has been the obvious disparity between theory and practice. Good practice cannot be based on faulty theoretical premises, and students are increasingly and quite rightly asking that the rational basis of their studies should be explained and discussed. Let us, however, turn for a moment to the practical considerations which also have to be taken into account when discussing the position of the history of education in colleges and departments.

In the first place, the time which can be given to the history of education in any college or department is necessarily limited. The other aspects of education dealt with in this book, together with teaching practice and (in the case of the colleges) the study of other academic subjects, have all somehow to be fitted into the timetable. One would certainly hope that the opportunity to study the history of education would be provided at every stage of the course and not telescoped into a single year as occurs in some colleges, but even so there are practical limitations to what can be attempted. A further point, which applies equally to the other disciplines of education, is that most students will not have had much, if any, previous experience of studying the subject. It is true that in university departments graduates in history and increasingly in sociology are fairly numerous, but there is something to be said for advising graduates in these disciplines to put their main effort during their year of professional study into other aspects of education of which they will probably know little or nothing. At any rate, it is clear that the majority of students will be approaching the history of education for the first time and frequently with only a very hazy recollection of such general historical background as they may have been taught at school.

The study of the history of education has, therefore, to be undertaken in a limited time and with students who on the whole have no previous experience of the subject. To state the position baldly like this is to invite the rejoinder 'Then why bother?' That, however, would be far too defeatist an attitude. Readers who have had the task of condensing a large body of material into essay form or who have had to explain complicated circumstances to another person not already acquainted with them will know that the need to condense material can act as a stimulus to clear exposition: the essentials have to be picked out and the main gist of the matter given in short compass. This is the situation which faces the lecturer in the history of education. He has to have not only a thorough knowledge of the subject himself but also the capacity to select really significant points and to make suggestions on how students may follow them up for themselves. He must stimulate interest but also give each student the opportunity to follow his own bent. This suggests, in very broad terms, that any course on the history of education should allow time both for the lecturer to introduce essential points and for the students to pursue particular aspects which interest them by private reading and subsequent seminar or essay work.

If we ask what are likely to be considered essential points by the majority of lecturers, we will probably find that recent historical developments provide the principal field of study. An attempt will usually be made to show how the present educational system in this country came into being and the main stages by which what is strangely called 'universal education' has been achieved. The danger here is that, as in the past, a chronological and narrowly institutional treatment will be given, with inadequate attention to the underlying movements in society which brought about the administrative changes with which most of the textbooks also deal. For example, it is not enough (though it may be important) to know the main clauses of the Education Acts of 1870, 1902 and 1944. But why were these Acts passed in the first place? What sections of the community benefited from them? What changes in social habits did they reflect and in turn influence? And did the curriculum, the content of which has never been laid down by Act of Parliament, go on developing independently? These are the kind of questions which need to be considered if the purely legislative changes are to have any real meaning.

A potentially more fruitful approach, which is being followed in an increasing number of colleges and departments, is to consider selected contemporary problems in a historical context. This approach has the great advantage of engaging the initial interest of students who will already have some acquaintance with the contemporary situation. There are, however, a number of pitfalls of which to beware. An immediate interest in, and certainly a detailed knowledge of, contemporary educational problems cannot always be assumed, and there is also a danger of projecting current controversy into the past, which can result in far too selective an account of the ways in which contemporary problems have developed. It is essential, especially when dealing with very recent history, to make the effort necessary to understand the points at issue as they were perceived by the people facing them at the time. It is said that no news is so stale as that contained in yesterday's newspapers, and there must obviously be limits to the extent to which contemporaneity should be the aim in any course on the history of education.

When this has been said, however, it remains true that live issues ought to be the ones to which students' attention is first directed. What are the 'live issues' which can most profitably be considered historically? At the top of the list must surely come the study of 'progressive' education, its historical antecedents, its practical consequences and the nature of the opposition to it. In recent years there has been a polarization of educational opinion which (leaving aside the cruder attempts to see the issues involved in terms of black and white) nevertheless represents a fundamental cleavage in the development of societies and of people's attitudes towards education. At a time when philosophers of education seem to be turning their backs on the educational thinkers of the past, it is essential for historians to look again at what has been written and to trace the connections which clearly exist between the ideas advocated in the past and the society which produced them. It will be found that many of the ideas now current, both 'egalitarian' and 'élitist', have a long history, and much may be learnt from studying their impact on previous generations of children and adults.

There are many other issues which are better understood by

bringing to bear the skills of the historian. Thus there has been much discussion recently of the need for curriculum reform, yet hardly any cognizance has been taken of the many previous attempts to reform the curriculum of schools and colleges. Why is it that, out of the immense range of human knowledge, certain parts have been stressed at some periods and quite different ones at others? Why have some previous attempts to change the curriculum been almost total failures while others have met with surprising success? Above all, to what extent does tradition determine what children and young people are expected to learn? A study of changes in the curriculum indicates that very often the efforts of reformers have not had the expected results and that considerable distortions occur between the first formulation of a new field of study and its introduction into the schools. We may instance the effect of the work of the German educationist Froebel on the infant schools of this country, into which his ideas finally penetrated towards the end of the nineteenth century. The 'kindergarten occupations' which Froebel had worked out in a very different context were slavishly imitated in many elementary schools and were utterly debased in the process. And how did it come about that the parents of the new industrial and commercial middle classes of the mid-nineteenth century often wanted their sons to receive a classical education, even though the study of the classics was at a very low ebb in most grammar schools and seemed to bear little relation to the needs of the new industrial society? The study of curricular changes in the past does not lead to an uncritical respect for tradition: rather, as one writer has recently put it, it 'prepares us for surprise in the nature of the movement of society'.[6]

Let us consider two other topics which could well form part of an introductory course in the history of education. First, there is the question of raising the school leaving age from 15 to 16 and, related to it, the assumption that another pressing problem – the need to reduce the size of classes – will have to be deferred because, according to this line of reasoning, not enough teachers are available to carry out both these changes at the same time. It is generally known that the idea of compulsory elementary education began in the nineteenth century and that the minimum leaving age has been raised by stages – in fact, from 10 in 1880 to 11 in 1893, 12 in 1899, 14 in 1921 and 15 in 1947. Is one to assume that further increases in the minimum leaving age are merely a question of the passage of time or perhaps are to be related simply to the changing demands of the economy? How far is the State justified in extending the principle of compulsion when many of the young people concerned do not appear to want it? These are important questions to which solutions have to be found, and there can be no doubt that a study of past experience in dealing with these same problems can be of great help.[7] The historian, though he does not claim to predict future events, can clarify the points at issue by considering their antecedents.

Similarly, if we consider the question of the size of classes, we may ask why it is that since the Second World War it has been thought that 40 should be the maximum size for a primary school class and 30 for one in a secondary school. There is in fact no educational reason why the larger class size should be considered more suitable for younger children, and a drive has recently begun to reduce the size of classes in primary schools to 30 also. But even this figure of 30 is a purely arbitrary one. At earlier periods one can find evidence that both much smaller and much larger classes were usual in schools of varying types. A great deal depends simply on the amount of money allocated for the employment of teachers and on the actual size of the classrooms provided in school buildings. It is only in the last few years that deliberate attempts have been made to provide rooms of varying size in new school buildings, for it is increasingly coming to be realized that while some activities may best be carried on in classes of 30 to 40 children, there are many others where small groups of children can work more effectively and economically in smaller spaces or where the best arrangement may be to provide separate booths for individual learning. The school buildings in use today were built at varying dates and in accordance with constantly changing ideas about how children should be organized for teaching purposes. A study of school buildings and plans can therefore shed a great deal of light on the development of teaching methods and the internal organization of schools, and such a study will show that there is nothing immutable or sacrosanct about the notion of 30 children to a class and no reason why class-teaching should not be modified for certain purposes.

A little earlier in this chapter we touched on the question of the 'relevance' of history and the pros and cons of studying contemporary or more remote periods. Without denying that in some circumstances the study of earlier periods can be of great value and interest, there would certainly seem to be a strong case for concentrating on the recent past in preliminary courses on the history of education in colleges and departments. In a sense, however, this distinction between the recent and the less recent past does not amount to much in actual practice. No student of history can escape from contemporary pressures and, as we saw earlier, the kind of history studied at all levels in our educational system has been greatly influenced by the outlook of the time: imperial history flourished when the British Empire was at the height of its power, diplomatic history during the inter-war period when there was renewed hope that the disputes between nations could be settled by international treaty, and so on. The student of education, especially one who has made up his mind to make a career in teaching, is naturally interested in the educational system as he finds it today. That is the contemporary aspect. But in order to elucidate points which seem particularly important now, it is often necessary to go further back into the past. For example, any discussion of the place of the English public schools in our present system of education must take account of the origin and development of these schools. This may well mean making some mention of, say, the foundation of Winchester and Eton in the later Middle Ages, and certainly we will need to understand how it came about that a number of grammar schools, apparently no different in origin from many others founded especially in the sixteenth and seventeenth centuries, came to occupy a dominant position and were able to maintain and often strengthen their independence of both local and national control. Such a study will not provide a universally-agreed answer to the 'public school question', but it will give the necessary background for intelligent discussion of the points at issue.

An increasing number of colleges and universities are adopting this 'topic approach' to the history of education. It has a great deal more to commend it as a 'way in' to the subject than the dreary chronological procession of facts which, by trying to include everything of importance from a given date to the present day, merely results in boredom and all too often in a complete absence of any understanding of the real influence of education on society. As the Bachelor of Education degree gains further momentum, however, and as other changes take place in the system of education for teaching, it is likely that more time will be available for a more comprehensive study of the history of education both at the undergraduate and postgraduate level. There is already enough experience of more advanced work in the subject to suggest that the problem-orientated approach should still be followed, since something has to be done to counteract the recurring tendency of history students merely to collect a mass of unrelated facts. This has been the bane of so many local studies, both in education and local history generally. Dr Finberg, in an amusing essay on 'How Not to Write Local History', has remarked on some parts of the monumental *Victoria County Histories* where the compilers have served up 'the contents of their notebooks in a kind of substitute for narrative' so that 'each fact is presented in a paragraph quite unconnected with the paragraphs before and after' or with some such transitional sentence as 'Things were no better eighty-five years later'.[8] Dom David Knowles has similarly commented on the indigestible mass of information given about monastic history in the older volumes in this series, and the same kind of remark could be made about many school histories written by members of staff as works of piety, not to mention some of the higher degree theses which gather dust on library shelves. The preservation and transcription of original source material are highly specialized activities of vital importance for further study, but they are activities which belong more to the realm of the archivist than the historian.

This is not to decry the value of local historical studies, properly undertaken. Indeed, there are several reasons why such studies can be of particular interest to students of the history of education. In the first place, there has been a strong tradition of local independence in English education and, as indicated earlier, a great deal has happened quite independently of any action taken by the central government. Indeed, until very recent times, and to a considerable extent even today, it was virtually impossible to make any generalizations about educational developments without basing one's conclusions on local examples. The difficulty is that as yet we do not have sufficient well-authenticated local examples on which to draw, and those which have been written up have all too often been treated as isolated phenomena unconnected with more general developments. How often does one find that school histories, for example, dwell in great detail on wholly commonplace occurrences but pass by, without comment, some really new development; or a higher degree student writes the history of the school board in some Victorian town without looking even for a moment at how the school boards in adjoining towns were tackling the very same problems in their areas. It is this comparative element which is often so vital – it provides points of comparison and contrast which stimulate further enquiry and can lead on to making significant generalizations based on valid data. Local studies also give the student the opportunity to study source material at first hand, which at least in some cases can have a very stimulating effect. One college student whose interest was aroused in nineteenth-century educational documents recently wrote that 'original source material has helped me to examine generalizations more closely and to develop a critical faculty which questions the validity of general texts and increases a desire for further research'.[9]

The comparative element need not of course be confined to local studies. Such studies perhaps appeal only to students with a particular cast of mind and certainly there are students who prefer to consider educational problems in a much wider context. One difficulty here is that many of the older books on what is called 'comparative education' tend to deal with educational systems in other countries in too contemporary a context. Either, therefore, the information supplied soon becomes out of date or the reader is given a detailed description of the present system with insufficient explanation of how it came to be as it is. It is good to note that the historical dimension is being given increasing weight in more recent books on this aspect of education, and certainly the stimulus of comparative study remains as a considerable virtue in this kind of approach. Two recent examples may be quoted, the first a study of the impact of the mission schools on certain Commonwealth countries and the second an American book on how the 'developed' countries may best help those which are 'less developed'.[10] Both these studies show what distortions occur when ideas and practices suited to one society are transplanted with the minimum of adaptation to other countries with very different traditions of their own. But a further significant point also emerges, since it appears that Western educational ideas often failed in other countries not simply because of the problems encountered abroad but because some of the Western ideas were not really sound to begin with. There is certainly much to be learnt from a study of the history of education in other countries and civilizations which would further contribute to an understanding of our own history and our present problems.

Several criticisms have been made in this chapter of some of the existing literature on the history of education, but there are many hopeful signs of improvement. In 1966 an excellent review was published of the literature on the subject (and of the place of the subject in education generally),[11] and subsequent additions may be noted in the lists included in the bulletins of the History of Education Society. Many of the printed sources available for the study of the history of education have recently been listed, and the scope of the important parliamentary papers on education has also been described; very useful selections from a variety of sources are also included in two recent compilations for students.[12] The manuscript sources are still largely unlisted and unexplored, and there is no doubt that the greatest need at the present time is for fully-documented studies of aspects and periods of the kind which, on a more introductory level, are being published as part of the Students' Library of Education.[13]

One regrettable feature of the literature on the history of education is the comparative neglect of the subject by historians working in other fields. In *The Oxford History of England*, for example, education is usually treated very briefly in one of the more general chapters on the intellectual and artistic life of the periods dealt with. Only rarely – as in A. L. Rowse's chapter on Elizabethan education in *The England of Elizabeth* (1950) – has education been treated as integral to the social conditions of the time. More surprisingly, economic and social historians have, with a few notable exceptions, tended to omit any detailed reference to the educational forces at work in society. The history of school buildings has similarly received comparatively little attention from architectural historians until quite recently.[14] Somewhat more encouraging is the note which is beginning to be taken of the educational aspects of urban development, as evidenced, for example, in H. J. Dyos's *The Study of Urban History* (1968) and D. Rubinstein's *School Attendance in London 1870–1904: a Social History* (1969). The Cambridge Group for the History of Population and Social Structure has turned its attention to the problems of measuring literacy, and the increasing importance attached to quantitative analysis (as in John Vaizey's books on educational finance) is having its effect on educational as well as other branches of historical study.[15]

The interaction between history and sociology, already alluded to, is likely to be increasingly fruitful, particularly perhaps in the field of the history of education, where, however, some reservations are being made about sociological methods.[16] Some suggestive ideas are, for example, included in W. A. L. Blyth's work on *English Primary Education* (1965) and Olive Banks has also made a notable contribution in her book on *Parity and Prestige in English Secondary Education* (1955). Scholars in the literary field can also make valuable contributions, perhaps the outstanding example so far being Philip Collins' *Dickens and Education* (1963). It has been suggested that what is required in studying any subject is the minimum amount of factual knowledge necessary to understand the relationship of that subject to other fields of knowledge, and this seems to apply with particular force to the history of education.[17]

We may therefore conclude that the situation so far as the literature on the history of education is concerned, though not entirely satisfactory, seems to be improving. The same comment may be made about the courses organized in colleges and departments of education. Enough has perhaps been said in this chapter to indicate that the field covered by the history of education is a very large one, but one in which students with interests of many kinds can work with profit. The history of education, properly conceived, is far from being hidebound by tradition and can be a vital liberalizing influence. The student of educational history is a student of change, and it therefore ill becomes him to hold tradition in awe. It can also be claimed with some justice that 'many of the methods and data that the historian of education uses, many of the attitudes and approaches he adopts as he studies the past . . . are relevant to the task that the teacher faces in becoming a better practitioner'.[18] The intellectual and imaginative effort required to understand the changes in our own society, and in societies other than our own, should help to produce the flexibility of mind which is needed to tackle the many problems which beset us now and will continue to beset us in the future.

Notes

1. See also R. W. Rich, *The Training of Teachers in England and Wales in the Nineteenth Century*, Cambridge University Press, 1933, p. 258f.
2. For two archive teaching units on education, see G. W. Hogg and J. C. Tyson, eds, *Popular Education 1700–1870*, University of Newcastle-upon-

Tyne, Department of Education, 1969, and A. H. Howlett, ed., *Education Act 1870*, Department of Education and Science, H.M.S.O., 1970.
3. Reported in *History of Education Society Bulletin*, No. 1, 1968. The secretary of the Society, which is also open to students, is Mr I. Taylor, St John's College, York.
4. The philosophical aspects are discussed in W. H. Burston, *Principles of History Teaching*, Methuen, 1963, and in W. H. Burston and D. Thomson, eds, *Studies in the Nature and Teaching of History*, Routledge & Kegan Paul, 1967.
5. For a discussion of the place of contemporary history, see D. Thomson, *The Aims of History*, Thames & Hudson, 1969, ch. 9; D. Heater, 'Contemporary History Justified' in *Teaching History*, Vol. I, No. 1 (1969); and Burston and Thompson, *op. cit.*, p. 107f.
6. E. G. Edwards, on 'The Need for a History of Higher Education' in History of Education Society, *The Changing Curriculum*, Methuen, 1971, p. 87.
7. These questions are more fully discussed in J. W. Tibble, ed., *The Extra Year: the Raising of the School Leaving Age*, Routledge & Kegan Paul, 1970, ch. 1.
8. H. P. R. Finberg and V. H. T. Skipp, *Local History: Objective and Pursuit*, Newton Abbot: David & Charles, 1967, p. 79. Cf. D. Knowles, *The Religious Orders in England*, Cambridge University Press, 1948, pp. x–xi.
9. This aspect is further explored in M. Seaborne, *Recent Education from Local Sources*, Routledge & Kegan Paul, 1967.
10. See B. Holmes, ed., *Educational Policy and the Mission Schools*, Routledge & Kegan Paul, 1967; and D. Adams, ed., *Education in National Development*, Routledge & Kegan Paul, 1971.
11. See B. Simon, on 'The History of Education' in J. W. Tibble, ed., *The Study of Education*, Routledge & Kegan Paul, 1966, ch. 4.
12. See C. W. J. Higson, *Sources for the History of Education*, Library Association, 1967; M. Argles, on 'British Government Publications in Education during the Nineteenth Century' in *History of Education Society Bulletin*, No. 5, 1970; D. W. Sylvester, *Educational Documents 800–1816*, Methuen, 1970; and S. Maclure, *Educational Documents, England and Wales, 1816–1967*, Chapman & Hall, 1968.
13. Edited by Professor J. W. Tibble and published by Routledge & Kegan Paul.
14. On this subject see M. Seaborne, *The English School: its Architecture and Organization 1370–1870*, Routledge & Kegan Paul, 1971; and *Primary School Design*, Routledge & Kegan Paul, 1971.
15. See, for example, P. Laslett, *The World We Have Lost*, Methuen, 1965.
16. The relationship between history and sociology is discussed in Burston and Thompson, *op. cit.*, ch. 1, and in articles by R. Szreter, in *History of Education Society Bulletin*, No. 3, 1969, and *University of Birmingham Historical Journal*, Vol. XII, No. 1, 1969. See also P. W. Musgrave, ed., *Sociology, History and Education*, Methuen, 1970.
17. Edwards, *op. cit.*, p. 95.
18. P. Nash, ed., *History and Education: the Educational Uses of the Past*, New York: Random House, 1970, p. 3. This book deals with a number of interesting problems from the point of view of the history of education.

5

The Philosophy of Education

R. F. Dearden

I

Philosophers have the reputation of not being the most practical of men. No doubt this supposed impracticality of philosophers is thought to be the inevitable result of their 'work' being done in the depths of armchairs. Certainly an armchair would not seem to be the best of positions from which to see what actually goes on in schools under the name of 'education'. Nor would so sedentary a person as a philosopher seem best suited to counsel and advise practitioners even about what ought to go on. People reputedly lost in abstract speculations do not immediately rush to mind as being amongst those best fitted to indicate how to cope with teaching French to 3C or how to cope with teaching reading to forty infants.

Indeed, if any person of a theoretical kind had something to offer to teachers, then surely it would be the scientist, and not the philosopher – or the historian for that matter. Curiously, however, even those armed with hard empirical research, still warm from the scientific hatcheries, may pale and shrink before the stern demand to show immediate practical relevance. And if the psychologist and the sociologist, sharing as they do something of the general prestige and glamour which attach to the sciences, can still be met by scepticism from practical men, such as busy teachers are, then what tiny hope can be held out for philosophy? Why should the professional preparation of practical men be additionally burdened by having to give some attention to philosophy, even if, as is often the case, it is only a very small attention? In the clamour of talk addressed to future teachers, need the voice of philosophy be audible at all?

Of course, it would be true to say, though hardly enough, that there are always some whose already existing puzzlement and perplexity more or less drive them to the study of philosophy. This is the only discipline that even attempts to answer the sort of questions that they are asking. In these cases, satisfaction of mind is sufficient reason to attend, and philosophy does not first have to promise advantages for concerns deriving their urgency from elsewhere. But anyone having a strong intrinsic interest of this kind is perhaps more likely to want to read philosophy as part or all of a degree course rather than to be content with it as just a small appendage to something else. In that case, a useful little book to consult would be *Philosophy: An Outline for the Intending Student*, edited by R. J. Hirst and published in paperback by Routledge & Kegan Paul in 1968. It is perhaps just worth mentioning, however, that there is a very small number of colleges of education which do offer general philosophy as one of the 'main subjects' which a student may choose to study primarily for his own personal development. Indeed, with the gradual introduction of philosophy into school sixth form studies, such a choice can even share in the direct relevance to the traditional school curriculum of the other, more usual, 'main subjects' of study.

But philosophy may claim attention in the preparation of teachers for reasons other than those of satisfying an already existing interest. In the first place, philosophy well taught has an important contribution to make in cultivating that critical attitude and rational temper of mind which will never be content simply to echo received doctrines or simply to acquiesce before the pronouncements of authority, but must screen before personally accepting. Education, in this respect probably like every practical field, has its share of dogmas, fashions, authoritarianism and now groundless traditions. Philosophy can help to produce an attitude of mind which is at least something of an antidote to this, even if it cannot give complete immunity to it.

There is a further advantage to be gained. This derives from the fact that we act as we do in the light of whatever beliefs we may have about ourselves and our situation. Practice is actually altered by theory, not always in immediate and particular ways, but more pervasively. The modification of our beliefs has important effects on our actions, and the modification of a teacher's beliefs about himself, his children, what he is teaching, how he is teaching it and why, will modify his practice, unless of course he is completely the creature of blind habit or has personal virtue squashed by the structure of his institution. To take a simple and trivial instance of the effect of belief upon action, we do not remain, even impatiently, at the bus stop after learning that the last bus has in fact gone. At a much more general and much less trivial level, we do not teach in the same way, or react to children in the same way, or expect them to learn quite the same things, when once we have come to see them in the light of different theoretical perspectives. Are children bundles of behavioural impulses to be shaped by conditioning, or empty minds to be filled, or self-directed inquirers in need of guidance? Are they responsible agents rather than the passive products of social and psychological circumstance, rational beings to be reasoned with rather than recalcitrants to be clouted? How the teacher sees it will make all the difference to what he does. And philosophy is one of several disciplines which are very relevant to how he will see it. But plainly something must now be said about the nature of philosophy as a theoretical inquiry, if this contention is to be made convincing.

II

Conceptions of what philosophy is are often of the strangest sort, no doubt chiefly because philosophy has been a discipline not normally encountered at school. People speak of their 'philosophy of life', of the need for a new 'philosophy of management', and so on. Faced with some particularly trying situation, we may be urged to 'take it philosophically'. But these ordinary usages are interesting for several reasons. First of all, it is not too difficult to find a relation between them and academic philosophy. In both cases an interest in generality and comprehensiveness of viewpoint is prominent. A person's 'philosophy of life' will consist of his general outlook, policies, priority-orderings and principles, and this is not at all far from some of the concerns of traditional moral philosophy, or ethics, especially as we find it in, say, Aristotle's *Ethics* or Mill's *Utilitarianism*. Even the equanimity that is called for in facing misfortunes by 'taking it philosophically' doubtless has some historical connection with stoic philosophy and the stoic ideal of apathy, or being indifferent to various normal entanglements with the world. Even the curious habit which public librarians have, of locating philosophical books as immediate neighbours of books on the occult, may be attributable to certain traditional philosophical concerns with appearance and reality, for instance with the question of whether the table as it really is can be identified with the table as it appears to us, mediated through sense perception.

There is, secondly, an interesting consequence for some forms of academic philosophy in the fact that several usages of the term 'philosophy' do exist in ordinary language. For it has been thought by some that academic philosophy is essentially a study of 'ordinary language', and that the concepts and distinctions to be found there are, as it were, basic controlling data for academic philosophy. But clearly this view is incoherent, because if it were true, then the nature of philosophy would be determined by the sense which 'philosophy' has in ordinary language, and in ordinary language the term 'philosophy' precisely does *not* mark out a study of ordinary language, but something along the lines indicated in the previous paragraph. Ordinary conceptions, then, do not take us very far in understanding what academic philosophy is, even though there may be discoverable connections or analogies between the two.

It might be thought that an obvious next step, now that the ground has been cleared a little, would be simply to supply the correct definition of philosophy as it is understood by professional philosophers. But there would be difficulties in doing that, and even objections to trying to do it, as much for philosophy as for any other discipline. Most likely such a definition would be the conscious or unconscious expression of a particular orthodoxy, surreptitiously legislating the correctness of its own approach. Even the more restricted field of the philosophy of education exhibits a variety of approaches, and this is even more true of general philosophy. Then again, no one can foresee what new developments will take place in a living discipline, so that no definition could be sure of allowing for them. In not allowing for them it might even come to exclude them as being wrong or as not 'really' being philosophy at all.

Historically, Western philosophy began with the Greeks, for whom it embraced virtually the whole of the disinterested pursuit of knowledge. Since then, one discipline after another has found its method, split off and become autonomous. Mathematics was the first and the human sciences are amongst the latest. Interestingly in this connection, the physical sciences are sometimes still traditionally referred to in universities as 'natural philosophy', indicating how they were originally a department of the parent discipline.

If the offering of a neat definition is not really possible, what one might do instead is to indicate a range of problems which concern philosophers or to point to certain classic texts which are paradigm examples of philosophic activity. But anyone acquainted with the texts would not need the explanation, while even a superficial look at such traditional problems as those of our knowledge of others' minds, the basis of moral and value judgments, the nature of beauty, the grounds of political obligation, the validity of the proofs of the existence of God and so on, would itself fill a book. Nevertheless, there are some general remarks which might be made about the nature of contemporary philosophy, at least as it is usually understood by English-speaking philosophers.

The first general thing that could be said is that philosophy is one form of the pursuit of *truth*. Philosophers wish to know the truth about the questions which concern them, and in that respect philosophy is more like science than it is like, say, painting or poetry. It is concerned to discover what is the case on some question, and not to construct or create something chiefly of aesthetic merit. And secondly, philosophy is concerned to seek out or establish the truth by the employment of *reason*. It is a form of rational inquiry in which the providing and the examining of arguments is absolutely central. Philosophy, therefore, is to be sharply distinguished from oracular pronouncement, the mere quoting of authorities, the stating of unsupported opinions or the bare feeling that something or other is the case. While a philosophical view may not be open to refutation by experimental counter-evidence, it will nevertheless be open to refutation through appropriate criticism of its supporting arguments. If they are invalid, then the view will probably cease to be of interest, though in a different way error can admittedly be fertile and instructive too.

A principal reason for continuing to study the history of philosophy is to become acquainted with the various forms of argument that have been discovered and the key moves that have been made on certain questions. Another reason why this history is still studied is that to ignore it will place one in constant danger of repeating or having to rediscover that history, and in more amateurish and undeveloped ways. Philosophy, then, is a rational inquiry aimed at the discovery of truth on certain questions. If it is the case that rational inquiry must itself be limited in its scope, and that other modes of access to truth are available to human beings, then that in turn is something which would have to be argued, and nothing in philosophy precludes a recognition of its own limitations.

A second general thing that is often said about contemporary philosophy is that it is 'second order' in character, or that it is thought about thought. Typically, much philosophy begins with the existence of a 'first order' form of understanding, such as mathematics, science, morality or the arts, and then proceeds to raise questions about this at a second level. It may be that conceptual difficulties lie in the way of a clear and adequate understanding of what is involved. For instance, what exactly is meant by 'God'? What is included in a true view of human nature? These sorts of questions are of the general form: What do you mean? How am I to understand this? Other sorts of difficulties arise over the objectivity of various kinds of truth-claim in the first order modes of understanding. How do you know that God exists? Is it by experience, by revelation or perhaps by some sort of rational proof? Again, how can you know what is right? Is this determined by how we happen to feel or by some 'intuition', or do we perhaps just decide it or ascertain it from what 'society' requires? These sorts of questions are of the general form: How do you know? With what right can you claim to be sure that it is as you say? Yet another sort of philosophical inquiry is into the presuppositions for something to be possible. How is it possible that a future occurrence can provide me with a reason for doing something now? What is presupposed in regarding individuals as responsible for their actions? And so on.

Conceptual inquiry in philosophy is not the stating of a definition, though in philosophy as much as in anything else it may sometimes be useful to stipulate or legislate what one will mean by some term. If a definition is to be the object, then it will be as the *outcome* of the inquiry. An inquiry into such concepts as those of space, obligation, personal responsibility or historical fact would aim at a clearer understanding of the concept in question or perhaps at showing that such an understanding is impossible because the concept is a confused one. Various moves might be made in such an inquiry. Different senses in which a term is used might be distinguished. For instance, teaching someone that something is the case is importantly unlike teaching a skill or teaching someone a habit or an attitude. Such distinctions may be important in considering the legitimacy of teaching religion in schools. Again, it may be important to demarcate a concept from some of its close neighbours, as for instance instruction from training, indoctrinating or conditioning. It may be that a concept needs to be placed in a network of related concepts to assist our understanding of it. For instance, the concept of knowledge may need to be related to belief, truth, evidence and meaning, or the concept of punishment to desert, justice, free will and responsibility.

Yet a further, and very interesting, sort of conceptual inquiry probes the presuppositions of having or learning or applying some concept. To take an example from a discussion of Wittgenstein's, how is it possible to point at something, say the colour of the pencil on the table? Of course, we typically point a finger at it, but how is that possible? How can I understand that that is what you are doing? In fact, familiarity with this action conceals a whole host of presuppositions, for instance that I can understand you to be pointing to the colour and not to the shape, size or materials of the thing in question, that I appreciate the conventions which constitute certain gestures and utterances of 'acts of pointing', that I am familiar with the 'language-game' involved and so on. One may need to try pointing something out to a baby before these assertions begin to seem plausible, so familiar are we with pointing. Yet a prodigious capacity for puzzlement by the very familiar is a characteristic quality in a great philosopher.

In teaching it is often very important to be sensitive to such presuppositions. What, for instance, is presupposed by the giving of an explanation to someone? Clearly, a statement of what is presupposed will include some reference to the satisfaction of his mind, but that is not enough, since he may be readily satisfied with what is false, or specious, or invalid. Therefore some objective condition has to be satisfied as well as the subjective one. Or take the asking of a question: what is presupposed by that? In general, one thing that is presupposed would seem to be a notion of what could count as a possible answer. This is obvious with highly specific questions, as in asking the time, but it will still be true of more general questions, such as those which open-mindedly inquire after causes. But a notion of what could count as a possible answer implies that we already have at least some understanding of the topic in question. If, therefore, a teaching method proposed to proceed by always starting from children's questions, probably on the grounds that interest would then be assured, then it would have to face the difficulty of how children were ever to be introduced to topics quite new to them. They would lack even a sketchy framework of relevant understanding of possible answers within which the right questions could arise. If we lack any understanding of mental illness, our questions about what is wrong with Smith will probably expect answers to the effect that he is tired, ate cheese before going to bed, will not pull himself together and so on. We just will not have the framework of understanding within which alone certain questions could arise.

Granted, then, that there are these various sorts of conceptual inquiry, perhaps an obvious next question to ask would be which concepts philosophers are particularly interested in, and why they find them puzzling or problematic. But I doubt whether anything useful of a general kind could be said about that. The alternative is the one chosen in this chapter of constantly giving examples. Furthermore, conceptual inquiry along the lines previously indicated is only one of the main sorts of way in which philosophers seek the truth. Another that was mentioned is that of inquiring into the grounds for various beliefs. Here again, philosophical interests are of a general kind. A philosopher would not be interested in why Smith should keep the particular promise that he made to Jones yesterday, but rather in why one should keep one's promises at all: what grounds are there for this general belief?

It may well turn out that different sorts of claim can be distinguished according to the different kinds of grounds that can be given. We all know that $5+7 = 12$, but what sort of grounds would be appropriate to that as a conclusion? Would you observe it to be so in numerous instances, or perform an experiment to show it, or just consider the meanings of the terms involved, or deduce it from some set of axioms, or what? Are mathematical claims just a special sort of formal logical claim? Are there, perhaps, some few basic kinds of grounds, the 'foundations of knowledge', on which valid claims of all other sorts rest or to which they are all reducible? Do some of the claims that we may have been inclined to make turn out, on critical examination, to be worthless or that kind of 'nonsense' that the logical positivists had in mind? Even some of our most familiar and commonplace kinds of knowledge may raise difficulties. Perception and even memory, for instance, may strike us as touchstones of reliability, yet both are liable to error and delusion. Or take our knowledge of other people's minds: what they are feeling, or what they intended in some action, or what they are thinking. How can we know all this? Is it an inference from facial twitches, movements of the limbs and vocal sounds interpreted on analogy with our own case perhaps, or do we have some more direct access to others' minds?

It would be misleading to give the impression that a few lectures on the philosophy of education, or even a three-year honours course in philosophy at university, would supply definitive answers on all these problems, so that all our doubts could yield to the pleasures of certainty. Inasmuch as progress is made in philosophy, it often consists much less in final or definitive solutions than in gaining a clearer view of just what the real question is or making a sharper set of distinctions in terms of which to formulate it. Equally, of course, one may well feel confident enough to frame some definite conclusions. And if certainty still remains elusive, then in that respect philosophy is not so very different from other disciplines, such as science or history, where theories and perspectives may change quite radically in a short period of time.

III

Most of what was said in the previous section was said in reference to general academic philosophy, rather than the philosophy of education more particularly. But there is no redundancy or irrelevance in that, since the philosophy of education just is general philosophy when it takes the theory and practice of education as a more narrowing criterion of relevance. The methods of argument employed, and many of the problems which they are employed upon, are common to both. In much the same way, there will be a great deal in common between educational and general psychology, or the sociology of education and general sociology.

The differences, so far as philosophy is concerned at least, lie more in the range and salience of topics of interest. There are some concepts of great interest in general philosophy, such perhaps as that of dreaming, which may be of no, or of no more than the most marginal, interest to teachers. Yet even in asserting this one may feel scruples that call for some qualification. Take the concepts of suicide and death, for example, both of great interest in ethics and the philosophy of religion. What relevance have they to a primary school teacher taking a class of forty vigorous and assertive nine-year-olds, or to a secondary school teacher about to discourse on the geography of the River Ganges or the irregularity of certain verbs? Yet the teacher is himself a person who acts within some framework of belief giving, or perhaps failing to give, meaning to his life, and something of this will be taught too, even if unawares. And now concepts of suicide and death may begin to look less ridiculously irrelevant. But for all that, the professional preparation of teachers must take place within a limited time, and some priority-ranking in terms of central and peripheral relevance must be imposed on the topics chosen.

For practical purposes then, we can certainly say that some of the topics of great interest in general philosophy will not be amongst the most urgent to be studied in a professional course component of philosophy of education. By contrast, education and the practice of teaching raise topics for consideration which otherwise might not have attracted much philosophical interest. Examples which come to mind here include the concepts of play, interest, equality of opportunity and 'education' itself. Nevertheless, there is likely to be a large core of topics common both to the wider and narrower fields of philosophical interest, such as, for instance, freedom, responsibility, knowledge, fact, intelligence, reason and so on.

In giving some more concrete idea of the topics commonly studied in professional philosophy of education courses, one could proceed in either of two directions. One could indicate the range of educational topics which require some clarification from general philosophy and which provide a criterion of relevance in going to the general discipline, or one could indicate those areas or branches of general philosophy which are likely to have the most obvious bearing on education. Both approaches have validity, and they do not precisely overlap. In fact, a situation arises here similar to that concerning, say, mathematics teaching. Some have thought that mathematics can be taught just as the need for it arises, in pursuing interests or engaging in project work. But though this approach has some validity, it is finally insufficient, because understanding mathematics has a certain logic of its own such that one thing presupposes another and requires to be taught in a fairly systematic way. In the same way in philosophy, starting from obviously relevant topics has the motivational advantages of interest but is insufficient by itself: there are interconnections with other parts of philosophy which need to be seen, and which can only be brought out by some fairly systematic treatment. The two approaches are doubtless both to be found in the best courses, and some illustration of each will next be given.

To take first the particular problems, topics or concepts on which philosophy may be some help, these can perhaps usefully be grouped together under three main headings. First, there is obviously the area of general aims and the principles of curriculum construction. Controversies here have arisen over general education versus specialization or versus vocational education. There are important value questions here to do with the worthwhileness of various curricular activities and the concept of an educated man. Putative general aims such as those of self-realization, character development, the education of the emotions, autonomy and growth need to be examined. There is also the currently very important question of whether the curriculum is to be thought of as differentiated in some way, for instance into 'subjects', or as 'integrated', perhaps around 'life-themes' or projects chosen on the basis of personal interest.

A second grouping of particular topics would be under the heading of teaching methods. Problems arise here in connection both with the content of what has to be learned and with the forms of social control which are to be exercised in the learning of it. There is a whole family of 'teaching' concepts, such as indoctrination, training, conditioning, instruction, imparting and explaining, which can usefully be distinguished, and their possible presuppositions and value connections can also be explored. The authority-relations characteristic of each of these processes, and their implications for the freedom of choice of the child, could be examined. There is a current fashion running against teaching of a direct sort, as in instruction, demonstration and explanation, and in favour of much more indirect and unobtrusive sorts of teaching, or 'learning management'. But how much *could* children 'discover' for themselves or hit upon by individual insight? How much children do, or do not, find out for themselves is a question for research, but it is for philosophy to examine the notions of discovery and experience with a view to what they presuppose for their very possibility.

Yet a third grouping of educational topics would be of those related to organization. Under this heading one might include practices related to organization within a classroom or school, such as streaming children by ability and the 'integrated day', and practices at the level of administration of a whole educational system, such as those of having separate types of schools or a single type of comprehensive school. Questions to do with justice, social and educational efficiency, freedom of choice, equality of opportunity and democratic control loom large if a whole system is being considered. How are these principles to be understood, and what is their validity? Is democratic control simply a matter of majority voting and everyone's having a right to his own opinion? Is it perhaps a variously institutionalized attempt to moralize political control in relation to individual rights? And in what sense, if any, are we all equal, or ought we all to have the same opportunities? A little dry philosophical analysis could beneficially introduce more clarity and less rhetoric into statements made in these terms.

If, however, the philosophy of education is approached more systematically from the point of view of the main divisions within general philosophy itself – and there must also be something of this approach – then there are some four main areas of philosophy which seem to be of most obvious and direct relevance to education. These are: (1) ethics, as a study of both social morality in particular and of personal values more generally; (2) social philosophy, or the application of ethics to social institutions; (3) epistemology, or the theory of knowledge; and (4) the philosophy of mind, or philosophical psychology. Ethics is of obvious relevance, in connection both with moral education and with wider questions of justifying the value or worthwhileness of what is done. Social philosophy is especially relevant to organization, and particularly to the political organization of an educational system, though of course such concepts as those of authority do have an application at the classroom level too. Epistemology raises general questions relating to such concepts as those of knowledge, belief, truth, experience and discovery, but also more particular questions, or the same general questions in more particular forms, in connection with particular disciplines. In this way there arise the philosophy of mathematics, of science, of history, of morals, of religion and of art or, more widely, of aesthetics. And fourthly, the philosophy of mind relates to general problems about states of mind and consciousness, and to more particular mentalistic concepts such as those of intelligence, thinking, creativity, concept formation, activity, play, interest and imagination.

IV

Which of the two approaches is most evident in a particular course will naturally depend on many factors: the interest exhibited by students, the preferences and backgrounds of the lecturers, the logic of the case and so on. Estimates of the importance of philosophy in educational theory also vary. For some colleges, six lectures in a three-year course may be seen as sufficient, even generous, measure. Other colleges devote some part of every year of the course to philosophy, and perhaps also make it an option for part two of the Bachelor of Education degree. This wide difference in practice is unlikely to be apparent from college prospectuses, and the position may rapidly change even within a given college as staff change and new appointments are made. However, it could not be soundly argued from any point of view that the philosophy of education is more than one contributory discipline alongside of others. To use an image of Michael Oakeshott's, philosophy is no more than one of the many voices in the conversation of mankind, and in a conversation there is no place even for a chairman.

One assumption that has been made in this article is that although the approach to the philosophy of education may differ in direction or emphasis, nevertheless, whatever the approach, it will be of an analytic kind such as is characteristic of general academic philosophy today, at least in English-speaking countries. But this analytic style has not always been evident in college courses and is not everywhere favoured even now. Sometimes, for instance, philosophy of education has been taken to be covered by some variant on the theme of the history of educational ideas. And, indeed, it has often historically been the case that philosophers have had ideas or remarks to offer on education. Plato and Aristotle, among the Greeks, would be classic examples. Others too, such as Locke, Rousseau and Kant, have had thoughts concerning education. In the present century, such philosophers as Dewey, Whitehead and Bertrand Russell have also written on education, in Dewey's case extremely influentially.

There is certainly something to be said for this 'great educators' approach. In fact, some acquaintance with such classic writings on education as, for example, those of Plato, Rousseau and Dewey, must surely be regarded as a necessary part of any liberal programme of teacher training. But on the other hand, there are several reasons which make it seem inadequate for philosophy of education to be represented in the course only in this way. Some of the greatest philosophers, such as Spinoza, have had little or nothing directly to say about education. Others who have indeed written on education, such as Locke, have not done so on the basis of their philosophical views but just as intelligent and sensible men. Then, again, these historical writings may not be the best introduction to philosophical modes of thought because in them philosophical considerations are richly intermixed with considerations of other sorts, such as we would now perhaps recognize as being psychological or sociological. Often the applications to educational practice that are suggested rest in part upon the empirical knowledge and the social institutions of the time, though both have now been superseded. Rousseau, for instance, assumes a one-to-one pupil–teacher relationship which is economic nonsense now, even for wealthy families, so that no superficial study of what he has to say will do. General principles of more permanent validity must be disentangled, and that takes time, skill and patience.

Besides the 'history of educational ideas' approach, philosophy of education may alternatively be represented as a study of certain philosophical schools, or 'isms'. This approach is much more popular in North America, and to some extent also in Scotland, than it is in England or Wales, so it can perhaps be more briefly described. It is possible to group together philosophers in the history of the discipline in such a way that similarities of interest or method are emphasized sufficiently to warrant speaking of a 'school', or at any rate a movement or climate of opinion. Typical examples would be realism, idealism, pragmatism, and more recently, existentialism. So long as a sensitivity to individual differences is retained, this is much more obviously a philosophically valid approach. Philosophical argument is studied and engaged in, and there is not the same problem of first isolating and identifying philosophical amongst many other sorts of considerations.

Nevertheless, as part of a course of professional preparation, this approach also has its drawbacks. The chief of these is to see what its practical relevance is, for in starting from general philosophical positions there remains something of a gap to be bridged to the making of statements in any way relevant to the choices and decisions which a practising teacher is called upon to make. Perhaps there are valuable implications to be drawn from these 'schools', but in starting from them the necessary restraint of educational relevance does not make itself very strongly felt, in which case the interest of many students is likely to be small.

Further reading

Whatever the approach that is adopted, it cannot be pretended that philosophy is an easy subject, or that large numbers are ever likely to clamour for it. But if the difficulty lies in the nature of the case, rather than in inadequacies of the teaching or unimaginativeness of approach, then it just has to be faced. And not everyone is automatically disenchanted by finding a subject difficult. How difficult a study of the philosophy of education is likely to be, and what sort of interest or advantage it is likely to have, can at this stage perhaps best be gauged by the reader's looking for himself at some relevant books in the field. For example, there is Professor D. J. O'Connor's *Introduction to the Philosophy of Education*, published by Routledge & Kegan Paul and one of the first books to appear in the contemporary analytic style. At much the same level of difficulty, though of varying concreteness, there are Glenn Langford's *Philosophy and Education* (Macmillan), Professor Reid's *Philosophy and Education* (Heinemann), and my own *Philosophy of Primary Education* (Routledge & Kegan Paul). All of these are available in paperback editions. More difficult is the collection of articles edited by Professor Peters under the title *The Concept of Education* (Routledge & Kegan Paul), or his own *Ethics and Education* (Allen & Unwin). And for those who prefer an approach through the historical classics, there are of course Plato's *Republic*, Rousseau's *Émile* or Dewey's rather long and difficult but great classic, *Democracy and Education*. Many books of general philosophy are usually readily available in public libraries – provided that one does not find it too embarrassing to browse amongst books placed next to those on witchcraft and the occult.

6

The Relationship between Theory and Practice

Harold Entwistle

I

'It is a commonplace that the characteristic virtue of Englishmen is their power of sustained practical activity, and their characteristic vice a reluctance to test the quality of that activity by reference to principles. They are incurious as to theory, take fundamentals for granted, and are more interested in the state of the roads than in their place on the map.'[1] Whether, as Tawney supposed, this suspicion of theory is primarily an Anglo-Saxon trait is debatable, but there is little doubt that English teachers do frequently dismiss educational theory as largely irrelevant to their daily activity in the classroom. 'That's all very well in theory, but it won't work in practice' is a familiar reaction to educational theorists. Tawney obviously believed this attitude towards theory to be unsatisfactory: however good you are at building roads, it is important that they should be going to the right places. Similarly, it would seem sensible to ensure that when you are bringing up children, you should reflect on the sort of people you would like them to become, directing your teaching intelligently to that end. So there seems no defence at all for the view that well informed reflection upon education (i.e. theorizing) has little to offer the teacher.

However, before simply dismissing this rejection of theory as a fault in practitioners, we ought to ask how far theorists themselves should accept some of the blame for the fact that educational theory is so often discredited in the eyes of teachers. Perhaps there is something inadequate in the advice which is proffered to the practitioner. It is not that in some mysterious way good theory turns out to be impracticable: perhaps the theory is itself mistaken. To modify slightly Tawney's metaphor – it may be that the roads are satisfactory and are going to the right places, but the available maps are inaccurate and misleading. In educational terms, the parallel would be that teachers really know the secret of good educational practice but that neither they nor the theorists have yet learned to give satisfactory explanations of how the good teacher succeeds in the classroom. Thus, it would be useful to begin by looking for limitations in educational theory itself.

A major criticism by teachers would be that educational theory is often much too utopian in character. Theorists rarely seem to be talking about the real world in which teachers struggle daily with flesh and blood, and many of their educational prescriptions have a ring of fantasy rather than truth. For example, children are assumed to be saintly innocents, desperately keen to learn and impelled by an insatiable curiosity towards unending voyages of intellectual discovery. But in the experience of many teachers, a day spent in the classroom is sufficient to falsify this notion of children as naturally curious about the universe in which they live: in all too many classrooms the reverse seems to be the case. The concept of original sin seems nearer to the truth about the natural child than do notions of innocence or inborn curiosity. Words like disobedient, insolent, sullen, rebellious, heedless, selfish, lazy seem more accurately to epitomize the nature of childhood than curious, co-operative, diligent. Teachers probably prefer an account of child development somewhat closer to the Shakespearian insight upon childhood ('unwillingly to school') and look for a theory of learning which recognizes the need for sugaring the pill, dangling the carrot, goading the unwilling and so on. In making this sort of criticism of educational theory, teachers are really complaining that theorists rarely derive their 'laws' of learning and of child development from observations of children in classrooms. The theorists' child is a fictional goody-goody, a wishful creature of the imagination; or, if he builds his theory upon actual observations of children in learning situations, these are frequently either highly privileged and untypical children or they exist in private experimental schools often in small groups bearing little relationship to class groupings in maintained schools. Educational theory sometimes appears utopian simply because its research basis is in institutions which *are* near-utopias when viewed from the classrooms where most teachers are actually destined to work. Thus, one approach to a more realistic educational theory would be to undertake much more educational research in the crowded classrooms of the typical publicly provided school. No doubt this is rarely done because of the methodological problems it poses for the research worker. But in default of such classroom based research, we must expect to derive only limited insights from work in experimental schools, as experimentalists themselves sometimes warn.[2]

A second reason why we over-simplify educational theory so that it looks unrealistic to practitioners also relates to the point we have already made about educational utopianism. Not only do we talk as though children were perfectly motivated to learn; much traditional social theory of education assumes that we are rearing children for life in the best of all possible worlds. Society as it exists is pretty sordid and, as Rousseau insisted, the inhumanity in men is a reflection of the extent to which existing societies deprave their members. But (the theorists seem to be arguing) that is the whole point of education. If only we learn to raise our children in the right way (at present, 'We Teach Them Wrong'),[3] schools can become agencies of social change in the direction of the best life that men can envisage. So education is regarded as a crusade and some educational theories function as war cries or slogans.[4] Instead of considered judgments about day-to-day procedures in the schools, theorists seem to offer merely a call to arms.

Perhaps the essence of these criticisms of theory that we have made lies in the words of another writer who uses the metaphor of the map: theorists sometimes offer us 'maps of which there is no corresponding territory'.[5] Just as it is possible to draw imaginary maps of treasure islands and utopias, so it is possible to visualize self-motivated children learning in manageable groups in perfectly equipped schools servicing the best of all possible (though never actual) societies. But these are not the conditions in which most teachers work, and in rejecting theory they are asking for more accurate maps of the terrain which they occupy every working day. The implication, then, is that theories which are as accurate as possible a match with practical situations should be derived from observation of the phenomena in question. This is to say that good theory can really only be derived from practice.

Some contemporary philosophers have emphasized the primacy of the practical over the theoretical in human experience. As one of them writes: 'To exhibit the primacy of the practical in human experience and the need to transfer the centre of gravity in philosophy from thought to action . . . we should substitute the "I do" for the "I think" as a starting point and centre of reference.' On this view, theories which seek to explain human behaviour should begin from the facts of how people actually do conduct their lives. If they are to give satisfactory explanations of the learning and teaching processes in schools, educational theorists, like cartographers, are under an obligation to map their theories on as accurate as possible observation of the data which they seek to explain. There are dangers in generalizing from exceptional children in experimental schools, or in inferring child development from what we would like it to be, or in prescribing educational method on the assumption that most classes contain perfectly motivated children abrim with curiosity and with an appetite for civilized culture. So prescriptions for curriculum and educational method will look more convincing to teachers when it appears that theorists have taken account of the pressures on the classroom floor and of the compromises which are a necessary part of a teacher's daily transaction with children.

II

However, although there is undoubtedly bad theory, there is also a sense in which there never can be a perfectly applicable theory, that is, the theory–practice gap is not simply a matter of there being inadequate theoretical advice for the practitioner to go away and apply to his daily teaching routines. The fault may lie, not in the theory, but in the unrealistic expectations of practitioners of what even a good theory may be expected to do. Demands are made on theories for guidance which, in their nature, it is impossible for them to supply. There never can be a one-to-one correspondence between theory and practice, if by this we mean theory that predicts accurately every contingency in a practical situation. A theory gains its relevance to every conceivable case which it attempts to explain only by being an exact account of none of them.

This can be illustrated concretely by further recourse to the metaphor of the map. As abstractions, making exclusive use of symbolic representation, maps only offer a limited account of a particular geographical area. Depending on the scale, some natural and artificial features will not be marked at all. The symbol marking a town or city usually tells us little more than its location. Its shape and (within broad limits) its size will only be evident on a very large-scale Ordnance survey map. And indeed, any attempt to present a model of the earth on a plane surface has to make compromising distortions if it is to convey any information at all. So anyone exploring territory with a map must expect the unexpected. He may be pleasantly surprised at the things discovered on the ground which are not on the map or, like the teacher in the classroom, he may find himself at considerable loss or inconvenience when confronted with phenomena which the mapmaker was unable to detail. So whilst we expect that maps will give us important guidance in understanding our physical environment, we do not complain (unless it is obviously a poor map) that they leave a great deal unsaid.

Perhaps another example will help to underline this point we are making about the inevitable gap between theory and the real world of daily experience. In our school physics most of us learn that freely falling bodies accelerate at a speed of 32 feet per second. This should mean that objects dropped simultaneously from a similar height would reach the ground at the same instant. Yet any small boys attempting to replicate Galileo's experiment by dropping a stone, a rubber ball, a cardboard box and a feather from the leaning tower of Pisa would discover (what common daily experience suggests) that these objects would hit the ground in that order and that, initially the feather might even 'fall' skywards. But this discrepancy in the speed at which they fall does not falsify the law of acceleration of freely falling bodies. For this principle of acceleration is true only 'other things being equal', a condition found only in a complete vacuum. And the fact that in situations in which people are practically interested in acceleration there never is such a vacuum does not lead us to conclude that physics is good in theory but won't work in practice. It is of considerable practical importance that beneath the disorderly, idiosyncratic appearance of things there are patterns or regularities which make prediction and control of our environment possible, provided we can identify and measure the variables which inhibit the simple application of theories or principles. Engineers and others wishing to apply the laws of motion must calculate from the theoretical formulae of mechanics, applying corrections in terms of their calculation of the effects of the forces (e.g., temperature, air pressure, etc.) which modify our expectations as inferred from the physical laws, 'other things being equal'. Much the same point could be made in terms of the corrections, allowing for the real world (e.g., the existence of monopolies and government interference), which must be introduced into economic calculations, if the simple relationships which economic theory assumes to exist between supply, demand and price are not to be a misleading account of real market conditions.

Educational theory, which makes considerable use of the behavioural sciences, is similarly destined to offer only generalizations which, viewed from practice, must wear the complexion only of 'half-truths'. Thus, predictive generalizations about classroom practice can only ever have the status of 'do this and that will probably follow, other things being equal' – whether our theories are about teaching methods, the development of intelligence and other personal characteristics, ways of keeping order in the classroom, the effects of different kinds of punishment, the function of interest in motivation and so on. If theories are only valid other things being equal, it is never an adequate refutation of theory to demonstrate its inappropriateness in *this* particular situation. Yet theorists (who have sufficient other shortcomings to answer for) are often also condemned because they fail to provide practitioners with detailed instructions for solving their own peculiar classroom problems. Drawing an analogy from our examples of physics and economics, educational generalizations have to be corrected in terms of the peculiar applied situation we have in mind. The precepts that children are best motivated to learn when appeal is made to their interests or the assumptions of progressive educationists that teachers fail only when they do not nourish the child's insatiable curiosity and irresistible desire to learn seem principles which have the sanction of common sense. Yet these and other almost self-evident educational axioms seem to break down on the classroom floor. The remedy is not to cultivate a commitment to rote, repressive teaching methods on the assumption that children are not interested in anything and must be driven, even browbeaten, into learning what is in their best interests. Instead we have to study the variables – individual differences, sociological impediments to learning, commitments to different kinds of cultures, as well as the different conceptions of interest and curiosity implicit in different stages of learning anything.⁶ And it is clear that some of the more important variables which must be accounted for when applying theory to practice are not immediately apparent when looking at the classroom itself. There must be reference to what might be called contextual educational theory. For example, much of educational sociology appears to have no direct reference to the teaching process or to questions of curriculum and method. But children come in to schools from very different cultural and socio-economic backgrounds. And the child's sociological background will help to determine his interests, his disciplinary expectations, his perception of the relevance or otherwise of the school curriculum, his need for remedial teaching.⁷ The teacher who tries to teach as though his classroom were in a sociological vacuum is courting frustration, and the student of education who looks only for theory which has an obvious and immediate classroom 'pay-off' will obviously dismiss much of this contextual theory (e.g., philosophy, history and sociology of education) as irrelevant – interesting to theorists but a waste of time for the hard-pressed practitioner.

III

All this means that educational theories have to be applied in a much more active, thoughtful, creative sense than is implied in the notion of applying pre-digested instructions or advice. The application of theory to practice, instead of being an exercise in carrying out advice is rather an activity of learning to ask a variety of questions about practical situations with the guidance of relevant axioms or generalizations. On the general nature of all theory and what it means to apply a theory, the philosopher Kant had this to say: 'A set of rules presented in a certain generality and with disregard of particular circumstances is called a *Theory* ... the practitioner must exercise his *judgment* to decide whether a case falls under a general rule.'⁸ Another writer refers to the 'folly of applying the right theory in the wrong circumstances'.⁹ We have to learn not only rules, theories and principles, but also how to interpret and apply them appropriately, that is, some initiative is required from the practitioner in discovering the pertinence of theory to his own practice. The job of a theory is to evoke judgment rather than rote obedience. The application of theory to practice is the bringing to bear of critical intelligence upon practical tasks rather than the implementation of good advice. Here again, our notion of the primacy of the practical is valuable. Practice is primary in the sense that the classroom situation is substantially *given* to the teacher. He is rarely beginning from scratch (even with a new class) armed with ideas that can be applied to a practical situation without antecedents. The schools are institutions having a lengthy history, and over the centuries pedagogical practice has become well established. In the same way, an individual school is usually a going concern, and for all sorts of reasons a teacher entering a classroom for the first time will find that children, their parents, his colleagues, educational administrators and others will already have expectations of what good teaching involves. Or, as we have already implied, it may even be that children bring with them from their social environment considerable resistance to being educated at all. Thus, a teacher of educational theory would be foolish or dishonest to pretend that he could communicate to students a body of theory which, in any immediate sense, could transform a classroom by removing impediments to good teaching. The educational theorist who thinks he has anything to contribute to the practical training of a student would be wiser to see himself in the role of a coach and to teach students to analyse a particular classroom situation and their own performance as teachers, much as the football coach talks about a particular game and a player's strength and weaknesses in a particular context. It is out of practical performance, in seeking to build on a student's strengths and diminish his weaknesses, that theorizing pertinent to practice is most profitably carried on. In talking critically about a particular class or lesson, theorizing (in a fundamental sense of reflecting on practice) occurs.

Theorizing of this sort in the classroom situation may well begin as nothing more than the application of common sense insights. What went wrong in a classroom may be obvious to all concerned, and theorizing about this may consist simply of giving common-sense judgments sufficient explicitness to drive the lesson home or generalizing so that the student is armed against similar contingencies when a similar problem arises in future. In terms of the parallel we have drawn between theories and maps, this theorizing as coaching is more like a traveller using a map to find out exactly where he is or how he went wrong, than of planning the details of a journey in advance. Our conclusion, then, is that the way into theory is through practical experience. The teaching of educational theory in lecture rooms apart from practical situations may itself give rise to mistaken notions of the use of theory and the way in which it can be applied to practice. The highly structured, ritual teaching of theory as a body of doctrine or 'law' may raise exaggerated expectations in students of what a theory can actually do for them in the practical teaching situation. If we teach theory ceremoniously in lecture courses apart from (and especially in advance of) practice, it may suggest to students that theories *are* things which they go away and apply as good advice. From the student's viewpoint, lectures in theory may look like a set of instructions much like the manual of instructions which comes from the garage with a new car. Unless it is made quite explicit that theory is a tool to analyse the classroom situation, it may be taken by students as a body of rules which, if properly implemented, will transform classrooms and schools overnight.

IV

However, our conclusion that teacher training should start with practice could look like a prescription to throw student teachers into schools at the deep end and let them sink or swim. And, as with learning to swim, it is possible that some potentially good performers are put off for life by this crude introduction to practice. Moreover, in terms of depth, turbulence and cross-currents, it is more difficult to keep one's head above water in some classrooms than in others. Thus, although we have taken the view that theorizing will have most meaning for a student teacher as he is taught to analyse his own strengths and weaknesses in practice and develop his own explanations of what he is trying to do in a classroom, there is also good reason for having some theory in advance of practice if he is to make an intelligent, confident entry into practice and avoid the sort of mistakes which would discredit him entirely as a teacher. He must learn and attempt to apply some rules in advance if he is to avoid getting off on the wrong foot and producing a chaotic classroom situation. He needs a provisional plan of action and some idea of what he would do if certain very predictable problems should arise. In this respect, learning to teach may be compared with learning to drive a car. Most learner drivers do not go through a comprehensive course in theory when learning to drive. A series of driving lessons usually consists of periods of practice driving interspersed with critical, evaluative and explanatory comments (i.e. coaching) from the instructor. But the beginner must know a minimum of theory in advance. Much of his first lesson will consist of explanation of the car's essential instruments and controls. And to obtain a Provisional Driving Licence, a learner has to affirm that he is familiar with the Highway Code. This does not mean that he has memorized it and is capable of applying it as a book of instructions; but if the danger of a serious accident is to be minimized, the learner should be sure that he knows in advance the essential rules of the road and the meaning of the mandatory road signs.

This parallel between learning how to teach and learning how to perform manual skills (like driving) illuminates a further problem of applying theory to practice. Often, an expert performer deems it appropriate to teach a skill by serving as a model: he performs himself in order to show what is required. At certain points in teaching a skill this may be the most effective way of demonstrating how to do it. But it is also a familiar experience of the learner that when he tries to copy a near-perfect model, he still gets it wrong. An inexperienced coach or instructor may take this failure to follow his example as evidence of stupidity or lack of aptitude in the learner. But there is an important reason why a student may be unable to copy the example he is set. Even the best of performances and explanations inevitably omit something essential to the skill. Some of the elements of a skilled performance are unanalysable: as one philosopher has suggested, there is a 'tacit component' at the heart of every skill which eludes specification.[10] Something essential to skilled performance defies description. Again, this can be illustrated from the example of learning how to drive. Suppose a learner driver is having difficulty in changing gear, a quite complex skill which requires co-ordination of both hand and foot with accurate perception of traffic conditions and judgment about the appropriate speed at which to make the change. The instructor shows the learner exactly how it is done; the learner tries again and fails. But his mistake does not necessarily lie in failing to see exactly what the instructor does and trying but failing to make the same movements himself. The 'failure' lies in the instructor's inability ultimately to show or explain the whole of what he did when changing gear. For, essentially, the skilled driver's knowledge is in knowing how to co-ordinate the appropriate movements and perceptions so as to choose precisely the right moment to make the change. He has the *knack* which consists in doing several things instantaneously, and knack, by definition, is not communicable to someone else. It is the *timing* of skilled performance which cannot be communicated and which the learner must acquire for himself through practice. Or, in the case of playing the piano, it is a matter of acquiring the right *touch*. We distinguish between a mere player and a good player in terms of the latter's having a touch which the former lacks. Both may be equally good at reading music and the lesser player's fault is not necessarily that he hits the wrong notes. Apparently both players know what to do, but the good player has acquired the touch, and experience suggests that no amount of coaching can transform the player who lacks touch. Thus, whether we are concerned with learning how to drive a car, to perform an art, to practise a craft or master a game of skill, it is not enough to have accurate descriptions or model performances. It is not doing exactly what one is told or shown which makes for skilled performance but doing it exactly at the right time and with a sensitive touch.

Much the same is true of learning how to teach and, indeed, this constitutes a further reason why theory must always seem to let us down in practice. This can be illustrated by reference to a perennial problem of the inexperienced teacher, that of keeping discipline in the classroom – a teaching skill which more than any other is apt to draw the criticism that theories inadequately represent practical reality. Over time, teachers have developed disciplinary devices ranging from mild admonitions (the shocked mention of a child's name, for example) through a variety of sanctions or deprivations down to drastic measures like ceremonial flogging and expulsion from school. But (even allowing for the fact that some of these punishments seem morally repugnant and are forbidden by some local authorities) the problem of teaching a student how to discipline a class cannot merely be a matter of giving him a complete list of the punishments available to him. The frequent complaint that colleges of education fail to teach students how to get and keep discipline cannot really mean that teachers of educational theory are unable to think up appropriate disciplinary measures to teach their students. If learning to keep discipline were just a matter of knowing available punishments, the matter would be simple. But the fact is that even someone who knows how to discipline children must necessarily fail adequately to teach this skill because, in the last resort, keeping discipline is not a matter of being familiar with available punishments, but of applying the correct sanction at the right time with the appropriate degree of firmness. This is to say that with discipline, as with the other techniques we have noted, 'timing' and 'touch' are the very core of success. With advice about discipline (as with other sorts of advice) the trainee teacher often complains that he faithfully followed suggestions, but these did not work. He seems to be dismissing the advice as bad advice and to be asking for a more satisfactory formula. But it is not so much that theorists give bad advice about discipline; rather it is impossible to give advice on exactly *how to time* a disciplinary intervention into a lesson. The successful disciplinarian does not simply know more disciplinary tricks than the poor disciplinarian. He has a sensitive perception of any classroom situation, born of his experiences in a multitude of daily encounters with children and by virtue of which he applies the appropriate rules and procedures at exactly the right time and with just the necessary emphasis. An adequate account of why a good disciplinarian succeeds in the classroom must refer not merely to the intrinsic merits of the things he actually does, but also to his experience. To the question, 'What exactly would you do to the boy who is insolent in the third row?', the experienced teacher will answer, 'It depends.' This is to acknowledge that every disciplinary encounter is unique, that his response must be related to the total context in which a disciplinary problem occurs and that, in any event, this response will be to a total situation which would be difficult to analyse in detail. Ultimately, then, success in the classroom is a matter of experience, and it is recognition of the fact that experience is not teachable which leads to the widespread conviction among student teachers that teaching practice is really all that matters and that courses in educational theory could be drastically pruned without loss.

However, despite our emphasis upon the primacy of practical experience over theoretical teaching, it is important to recognize that practical experience, of itself, is an insufficient teacher. One reason for this ultimate inadequacy of mere practical experience is that any practical situation is limited in place and time. In a different classroom situation, different strategies might be appropriate, and students ought to be trained to generalize their insights and experiences in such a way that their skills are transferable to novel situations, either in different schools or in response to educational innovation. This is why the concept of theorizing as coaching in the practice situation can only be a part of the teacher's encounter with theory. As well as reflection on his own experience in a particular classroom, the initiate needs to be put into touch with the experience of others in different practical situations. To some extent, this can be achieved by arranging student visits to a variety of educational institutions. But ultimately, this widening of the student's experience and perspectives can only be achieved vicariously, and much of the literature of education consists of description and evaluation of the work of successful practitioners. Some texts of educational theory are also attempts to generalize from what seems to be successful practice in a variety of teaching situations, in an effort to articulate sound educational principles applicable to any educational situation. This sort of general theory is derived not only from observation of contemporary practice in the schools, but also gathers insights from the history of education and from comparative studies of education in other societies. As well as reminding ourselves that colleagues in other schools have different kinds of experiences (as well as common experiences), we have to confront the fact that at other times and in other places children are educated quite successfully using different methods and different types of institutional organization.

As we have implied, this reference of the student's theorizing to a wider range of experience than his own is needed partly because of the necessary temporal and spatial limitations of even the best of schools. But it is not unusual for students to find themselves practising in classrooms which leave a great deal to be desired as models for the development of their own practice. In some schools, both teacher and pupil morale is low, and practice approximates more to that of the Dickensian schoolmaster than to the best of contemporary practice; at best, learning is a rote assimilation of obsolete knowledge, and at worst, children are beaten or intimidated into compliance and spend their time in meaningless exercises whose only value lies in keeping them quietly occupied. If students are not to come out of this sort of situation justifying the methods they have observed (and may have been driven to use) as all that will work in practice, their attention has to be directed towards educational theory which refers to classroom practice which is educationally justifiable. It is not enough for a student to learn to come to grips with whatever 'successful' practice he discovers in the classroom. For example, we referred earlier to the problem of discipline and noted the existence of a wide range of possible sanctions for use against children. But learning how to discipline children is not merely a matter of discovering, through experience, which punishments are likely to succeed in particular situations. Some conceivable forms of punishment would have to be dismissed as morally repugnant. Others are a matter for controversy – corporal punishment, for example. One observer of a secondary modern school prompts the conclusion that many of the conventionally accepted disciplinary routines in schools are actually conducive to indiscipline in many children: it is apparent that some schools' disciplinary procedures produce their own 'delinquents'.[11] Moreover, to some teachers, the whole of our earlier discussion of discipline as a problem of punishment would be quite unacceptable, and the question we posed, 'What would you do with the insolent boy in the third row?' would be unanswerable. In many classrooms the problem of the insolent child simply does not arise. Discipline implies something altogether more positive in teacher–pupil relationships than mere class *control* with or without punishment. Good discipline is a matter of teaching children to come to grips with knowledge and skill so that the problem of the disorderly classroom rarely arises and the reluctant learner is only occasionally encountered.

Thus, coming to terms with classroom practice involves students in asking how far what they find is educationally defensible. Whilst resisting some contemporary condemnations of the school as an institution destructive of education, accounts of particular schools, such as those provided by Hargreaves and Partridge,[12] must give us pause before concluding that existing practices leave little to be desired and that if training establishments cannot make a better job of fitting students for conditions they will find in schools, they had better stop theorizing and leave training to the successful practitioner.

V

The point of this criticism of what is sometimes taken to be 'successful' practice is that educational theory also has a normative function to perform. Earlier, we conceded that some educational theorizing is unrealistically utopian. But the search for 'realism' in educational theory cannot commit us to approval of everything that appears to succeed in the classroom: some practices which seem to work successfully ought not to receive theoretical sanction. One would not have to be a categorical opponent of corporal punishment to condemn the classroom where good order was always a product of beatings, threats or appeals to fear. Apart from the moral dubiousness of this sort of discipline as such, it could be the case that obedience and order in a classroom were achieved only at the expense of learning. There are some classrooms where children sit perfectly still but do very little else, or where they are bludgeoned into rote activity which issues in little of educational value. Even 'successful' practices with long and respectable histories may need to be called into question. Until recently, for example, it was assumed that the only successful way to operate the English educational system was by streaming in primary schools and the segregation of secondary schooling on the basis of measured I.Q. So well did tripartite secondary schooling seem to work that to call it into question seemed a mere blasphemous criticism of the created order of things. Other nations (like the Americans) might manage with single-track high schools, but this was only the measure of their spiritual degeneracy and the poverty of their intellectual life. However, social theorists of education have come increasingly to question how well, or in what sense, 11+ and segregated schooling really do work. Perhaps this system was adequate to the task of throwing up an élite capable of servicing the first industrial revolution, but can we afford such waste of talent in the face of the different technological and social demands of the end of the twentieth century? At all levels in the educational system, examples could be multiplied of the way in which apparently successful practices only serve to underline the inadequacy of our cultural and social values. Hence, educational theory must have a critical and normative function. We have to submit our practices, both as classroom teachers and in terms of our larger educational arrangements, to the scrutiny of theory. With theories we evaluate our practice, whether they are empirically derived theories of learning and child development or philosophical assumptions about the good life. Unless we are very fortunate or complacent, such evaluation must act as a spur towards improvement. We are rightly suspicious of educational and social utopias which are so adrift from the world in which we live that they could only be achieved by a completely fresh start, probably requiring violent revolution in order to destroy the legacy of the past. But mistrust of utopias and utopian thinkers does not require that we complacently accept our existing arrangements as satisfactory or practically unalterable.

However, once we move into the area of normative educational theory and become concerned not merely with technical problems (e.g., the best way to teach long division or the history of the industrial revolution) but also with the ends to which we direct our teaching techniques, we find ourselves in controversies which cannot be resolved experimentally. If we could do sufficient research, we might reach a fair degree of agreement on *how* people should teach. But there is also disagreement on whether there is any point in teaching, for example, long division to the less able, or whether history syllabuses should include the industrial revolution – even whether history should lose its separate identity in the curriculum and (with geography) become part of a social studies synthesis. Perhaps one reason for the rejection of educational theory by practitioners follows from this fact that theorists often disagree amongst themselves and, in the spirit of 'a plague on both your houses', the teacher occupies himself exclusively with the daily business of teaching. But unless the curriculum is to ossify and remain insensitive to the changing interests of men and unresponsive to technological development, or unless our educational arrangements are to be a mould into which we force all children irrespective of their individual strengths, weaknesses, abilities and talents, we cannot avoid stepping into this controversial area of concern with educational norms and values. And it must be recognized that theoretical disagreement at this level is only a reflection of our uncertainty about what constitutes the good society, what it means to be an educated person and, hence, what are worthwhile curriculum activities. It is true that in some educational systems these decisions about curriculum content are made outside the schools, at a national level, by committees of the Ministry of Education. In the Scandinavian countries, for example, every teacher is handed a book of teaching plans where content of the various subjects is outlined in some detail for each grade; the proportion of time to be devoted to the teaching of each subject is also specified. There are those who believe that this method of achieving consensus upon curriculum content is to be preferred to the normative anarchy which exists in the English educational system, where, for good or ill, the individual teacher has the freedom to derive his own curriculum in consultation with his headteacher.[13] Of course, perceptive foreigners do point out that the English teacher's vaunted freedom is more shadow than substance. They refer to the uniformity imposed upon schools by examination requirements (11+ and the secondary school examination boards). It is also true that aside from these examination pressures, historical factors have made for uniformity in curriculum development, so that, for example, although in principle there is no reason why every school should not have a unique history syllabus, research would probably reveal a high common content in the history teaching in different schools.

However, it would be a mistake for the practitioner to fall back on the fact of these historical and examination factors which seem to dictate the curriculum as reasons for not himself engaging in critical reflection upon what he finds himself doing in the classroom. For it is precisely the historical sanctions and examination pressures upon the curriculum which are taken to be sources of irrelevance and sterility in contemporary education – witness the fact that one source of opposition to 11+ was those who deplored its unfortunate backlash on the primary school curriculum. Thus, to free education from the dead hand of tradition and to devise liberal examination procedures like CSE Mode III (an internal examination, externally assessed, of a curriculum arising from the interests of the children and their teacher)[14] would be to require greater initiative from the teacher and the exercise of his latent freedom to teach as and what he thinks is in the best interests of children.

But exercise of this freedom requires personal integrity in the teacher, an awareness of the findings of educational research and the problems and values at issue in the educational debate, which demand a high level of personal education and professional competence, the latter involving an ability to scrutinize practice in the light of 'the best that has been thought and said' in the field of educational theory. Existing theory may be unsatisfactory, and the discovery that, by its nature, theory cannot give us all we desire (in the sense of providing ready-made specific answers to particular questions) may lead some practitioners to conclude that, being themselves active and non-reflective by disposition, they will leave the theorizing to others – to the dreamers or the talkers who are good at it and find it rewarding for its own sake. But the implication of drawing such a conclusion should be clear. It is a rejection of any obligation to think purposefully and intelligently about how and why we educate our children. Like Tawney's roadmakers, it is to be involved in busily constructing something which nobody might ever want to use. Indeed, following from what has just been said about the English teacher's freedom from central direction, it is a paradox that, belonging to a people whom Tawney believes so curiously uninterested in maps, it is he who most needs the capacity to read and interpret the maps provided by educational theorists.

Conclusion

Though sympathetic to the practitioner's dismissal of much theory as irrelevant to his work, the writer of this paper is not anti-theory but, on the contrary, committed to the view that we need ever more pertinent reflection upon the processes of education. And the way to a more practice-relevant educational theory does not only require that educational theorists mend many of their ways. It also needs considerably more commitment to theory than many practitioners have hitherto displayed, not merely as a means towards teaching theorists their proper responsibilities to produce credible theory, but also because, as we have argued, ultimately even good theory only gains relevance in and through critical application.

Notes

1. R. H. Tawney, *The Acquisitive Society*, Fontana Library, 1961, p. 9.
2. An elaboration of this and other issues raised below can be found in Chapter 11 of H. Entwistle, *Child-centred Education*, Methuen, 1970.
3. Sir Richard Acland, *We Teach Them Wrong*, Gollancz, 1963.
4. See I. Scheffler, *The Language of Education*, Springfield, Illinois: C. C. Thomas, chapter 2.
5. S. I. Hayakawa, *Language in Thought and Action*, Allen & Unwin, 1952, p. 255.
6. Consider, for example, the varying emphases upon pleasure, play, discipline, drill and hard work required by Whitehead's principle of rhythm in education, comprising stages of romance, precision and generalization; see

A. N. Whitehead, *The Aims of Education*, Williams & Norgate, 1955; see also my own brief explanatory note on this principle, Entwistle, *op. cit.*, pp. 213–17. Note also the naïve concept of interest in much contemporary educational discussion as compared with classic statements of the principle in the writings of Herbart (*The Science of Education*, Swann Sonnenschein, 1897) and Dewey (*Democracy and Education*, Macmillan, 1961 ed.).

7. See Entwistle, *op. cit.*, pp. 190–4.
8. See the essay 'On the saying "That may be all right in theory but is no good in practice"' in G. Rabel, *Kant*, Clarendon Press, 1963.
9. B. Crick, 'The Introducing of Politics', in D. B. Heater, ed., *The Teaching of Politics*, Methuen, 1969, p. 12.
10. M. Polanyi, *Personal Knowledge*, Routledge & Kegan Paul, 1958.
11. D. H. Hargreaves, *Social Relations in a Secondary School*, Routledge & Kegan Paul, 1967.
12. Hargreaves, *op. cit.*; J. Partridge, *Life in a Secondary Modern School*, Penguin, 1968.
13. F. Musgrove and P. H. Taylor, *Society and the Teacher's Role*, Routledge & Kegan Paul, 1969. See this text for a criticism of the English teacher's autonomy in determining the ends of education.
14. See *The Certificate of Secondary Education*, Examinations Bulletin No. 1, H.M.S.O., 1961.

7

Curriculum Courses

J. W. Tibble

In all colleges of education the total course is made up of three ingredients: (1) The study and practice of 'education', which is concerned with the students' professional education; (2) one or two main or special studies, which (except in the case of students preparing for specialist work in secondary schools), are studied with personal and cultural rather than professional aims in mind; and (3) what are most commonly called 'curriculum courses', though there are many other names for them.

This book is chiefly concerned with the first of these ingredients; the reason for including in it something about the third is indicated by a reference to the Ministry of Education pamphlet *The Training of Teachers*, 1957:

> The Curriculum course should on the one hand give students the experience of learning something new, at their own intellectual level, in order to help them understand what this experience means to children, and on the other hand, of studying closely, if not extensively, examples of work actually carried out by children. Unless the Curriculum course is an amalgam of the students' personal and professional education, it is hardly likely to serve its purpose.

The term 'curriculum' is used for these courses by about half of the colleges of education. Some colleges call them 'professional' courses, and other terms used are 'background', 'basic', 'general', 'college', 'subsidiary' and 'method' courses. Many colleges refer to basic and general courses as well as curriculum courses. These basic or general courses are usually in English and Mathematics with, in some cases, divinity (or religious education or religious instruction) and physical education also included. The number of curriculum subjects studied also varies greatly, usually more being required of those preparing for work in primary schools. The courses also vary in length, short introductory courses often being taken during the first year, others taken for a whole year or longer. Some of the courses are optional and others compulsory. Some colleges concentrate more on the method of teaching a subject; in other colleges more emphasis is placed on content. Some colleges attempt to cover briefly all subjects which are part of the primary school curriculum, whereas other colleges allow for more selection. There is also considerable variation in the relationship between curriculum courses and the other two sections of the total course, e.g., in whether education tutors or main course tutors or both are responsible for the curriculum courses, or in whether a main course includes consideration of teaching methods.

Most of the descriptions of these courses in college prospectuses do, however, contain some reference to the professional training aspect, as the following phrases indicate: 'closely associated with practice in teaching', 'to bring them into touch with the needs of children and the requirements of the curricula of the schools', 'in preparation for their teaching responsibilities', 'to give the necessary background and professional study for teaching the subject in schools', 'to familiarize the student with the purpose and method and to some extent the content of the subjects which they may be required to teach', 'concerned with the teaching of the subject and with increasing the students' own knowledge'.

It is interesting to note that in the nineteenth-century colleges and pupil teacher centres, these curriculum courses made up the greater part of the total certificate course. What the pupil teacher or student was mainly concerned with was mastering the subjects of the elementary curriculum to a point well beyond that of his likely oldest and brightest pupil; he was also learning through practice and precept the methods of teaching these subjects as 'lessons' in the 'simultaneous' system of class organization. When, after 1902, the intending teacher's general education, the mastery of the subjects, was handed over to the grammar schools, it made it possible for the colleges (a) to develop more advanced specialized courses in the curricular subjects and at the same time reduce their number to one or two main subjects and (b) to develop, as is described in chapter 1, the study of education out of the meagre professional content on the theory side of the nineteenth-century course.

As these new aspects of work developed, they naturally demanded more time for their study and, as a consequent, the time left for the curriculum courses shrank to a third or less of the total course.

This would seem reasonable enough, if, in fact, as was the original intention, the students' pre-college education equipped them, on the content side, over the whole range of the primary school curriculum. The college curriculum courses could then concentrate mainly on the professional aspects of teaching these subjects. Unfortunately (for this purpose), the tendency to specialize, which we have noted in the college, developed equally strongly in the secondary schools from which the students (and their tutors, too, for that matter) were recruited. As most of you who read this will know from your own experience, this means that many subjects are dropped at some point in the secondary course so that the student can concentrate on those chosen for advanced study in the sixth form. After a gap of three years or more, much revision and remedial work is needed before a student can make progress, even if the assumed starting point for the course is no higher than O level. The problem facing the colleges is obvious enough: the time available for curriculum courses is just not enough to cover both content and method over the range of the primary curriculum.

The only satisfactory remedy for this is a drastic revision of the secondary course, making it possible for a student to pursue a broad range of studies up to the age of eighteen. Though this is the practice in a good many other countries, and the need is well recognized here, so far all attempts to broaden sixth-form studies have failed. The reasons for this are the nature and length (normally three years) of the university courses in this country and the intense competition for entrance to them. In this situation, the grades obtained in A level examinations are deciding factors; and the way to achieve the highest grade possible is intensive coaching in the subjects being examined. Even if this is defensible for the students who go on to take a one-subject honours course at a university, it does not seem right that the many who would benefit from and actually need, as we have seen, a more broadly based course should have the same treatment.

Given the problem and that a satisfactory solution of it requires changes in the pre-college course, can the colleges do more and better in this field within the scope of their own courses? It is generally agreed, for the reasons given above, that curriculum courses are the least satisfactory part of the total course, mainly because there is inadequate time, assuming that less than a third of the total time is available, for the job that has to be done. It will work out, at best, at about an hour a week per subject. A good many colleges give more time to curriculum studies in the earlier part of the course, particularly on the content side. In subjects like mathematics, many students have negative attitudes to the subjects dropped at an earlier stage, and what is needed is re-learning from scratch. There is also the problem that, in some subject fields, revolutions have taken place in the ways they are now presented to young children, and these will be new to the students. Some colleges have restructured the college's curriculum in the first year of the course, so that it corresponds with the primary curriculum in range. This means, in effect, getting rid of the names 'Education' and 'Main Studies' in the first year; in subsequent years the student gradually reduces the width and chooses some aspects for study in greater depth. The objective is to combine the necessary width with optional studies in depth over a longer period. This also allows for some variations in the proportions of width and depth according to the students' needs.

This is all the more necessary because primary schools and secondary schools are, in fact, organized in quite different ways; in the former a teacher is responsible for nearly the whole range of studies of a class of children – which may be a stream of a year group, or a mixed year group, or in some cases mixed from a two-year range – and in the latter a teacher normally is responsible for a subject with a number of mixed or streamed groups. The coming into existence of some middle schools which straddle the primary–secondary cleavages introduces the possibility of a third variation, combining general practitioner with some degree of specialization. What some colleges are proposing in the way of modifications of their curriculum should produce a more flexible teacher. It has for some years now been a major irony that in a period when the colleges were being directed to produce, on average, 80 per cent of their output for the primary schools, the structure of the college curriculum was more appropriate for producing secondary specialists than primary generalists. Traditionally, the colleges were equally concerned with what happened on both sides of the cleavage. What we are seeing today is a reconsideration of the validity of the break at 11+, not only in terms of objections to selection procedures, but in questions about the normal forms of organization and the differences between them. We can accept that older children have different needs from younger children and that these differences should involve different forms or organization of schools; but surely the change from one to the other should be a gradual process over the years, not a sudden transition. If this is the case, it will require a good many teachers for the transitional stages with the combination of breadth and some depth which has been mentioned above.

Index

Abercrombie, M. L. J., *The Anatomy of Judgement* (1969), 29, 42
Adamson, J. W., pioneer of history of education, 13
Arnheim, R., *Visual Thinking* (1970), 29, 42

Bain, A., *Education as a Science* (1882), 7
Banks, O., *Parity and Prestige in English Secondary Education* (1955), 78
Banton, M., *Roles: An Introduction to the Study of Social Relations* (1965), 48, 63
Barnett, S. A., *Instinct and Intelligence* (1970), 28, 42
Bell, Andrew, on teacher training, 6
Bernstein, B., on language, 52, 63
Birley, D., and Dufton, A., *An Equal Chance* (1971), 59, 63
Blyth, W. A. L., *English Primary Education* (1965), 78
Boyd, W., pioneer of child study, 10
Boyle, D. G., *Student's Guide to Piaget* (1969), 35, 42
Brookover, W. B., *A Sociology of Education* (1955), 53, 63
Bruner, J. S., 23
Burt, Cyril, first educational psychologist, 10

Butcher, H. J., *Human Intelligence* (1970), 39, 42

Cattell, R. B., *The Scientific Analysis of Personality* (1965), 23-4, 31, 42
Child study, founding, 10; later work, 31-2
Clark, D. Stafford, *What Freud Really Said* (1967), 30, 42
Collins, P., *Dickens and Education* (1963), 78
Cross Commission, 13
Curriculum courses in colleges of education
  development, 115
  early specialization, 116
  modifications, 117-18
  purpose, 114-15

Dearden, R. F., *Philosophy of Primary Education* (1968), 94
Dewey, John, 13, 15, 94
Douglas, J. W. B., *The Home and the School* (1964), 52, 63
Dyos, H. J., *The Study of Urban History* (1968), 77

Education, study of
  contribution
    of educational psychology, 18-43
    of history, 64-79

Education, study of—*cont.*
  of philosophy, 80–94
  of psychology, 8–12
  of sociology, 12, 44–64
  early beginnings, 6–7
  history of education in, 13–14
  misconceptions, 2
  nature of the subject, 15–17
  philosophy of education in, 14–15
  recent changes, 2, 5
  relation of theory to practice, 95–113
  students' ignorance, 1
Evans, K. M., *Sociometry and Education* (1962), 57, 63

Fleming, C. M., on changes in child study, 11
Floud, J. E., and Halsey, A. H., *Social Class and Educational Opportunity* (1957), 12, 17
Freud, S., 19, 20–1, 29–30

Gagné, R. M., *The Conditions of Learning* (1965), 27, 42
Galton, Francis, 20
Gesell, A., *et al.*, *Child Development* (1946), *Youth: the Years from Ten to Sixteen* (1956), 32, 42
Getzels, J. W., and Jackson, P. W., *Creativity and Intelligence* (1962), 38
Gregory, R. L., *Eye and Brain* (1966), 29, 42

Hancock, A., and Willmott, P., *The Social Workers* (1965), 59, 63
Hardie, C. D., *Truth and Fallacy in Educational Theory* (1942), 14
Hargreaves, D. H., *Social Relations in the Secondary School* (1967), 57, 63
Hebb, D. O., *The Organisation of Behaviour* (1949), *Textbook of Psychology* (1966), 28, 42
Hirst, R. J., *Philosophy: An Outline for the Intending Student* (1968), 81
History of education
  aims, 68–9
  beginnings, 12–13, 65
  comparative neglect, 77
  comparative studies, 76
  contemporary problems, 71–2
  curriculum reform, 72
  later developments, 13, 66
  limitations, 69–70
  local historical studies, 75
  progressive education, 71
  raising of school leaving age, 72–3
  relations with sociology, 77–8
  size of classes, 73
  survey of courses in 1967, 67
  topic approach, 74
  trends in history teaching, 66–7
Hoyle, E., *The Role of the Teacher* (1969), 54, 64
Hudson, Liam, 24–5

Jackson, B., and Marsden, D., *Education and the Working Class* (1962), 12, 17, 52, 58, 64
Jones, L. G. E., *The Training of Teachers in England and Wales* (1924), 6, 17
Judd, C. H., *The Training of Teachers in England, Scotland and Germany* (1914), 6, 17

Kellmer-Pringle, M., *et al.*, *1100 Seven Year Olds* (1966), 52, 64
Kohler, Wolfgang, 22

Langer, S., 63, 64
Langford, Glenn, *Philosophy and Education* (1968), 94
Lippett, R., 24
Lovell, K. (ed.), *Educational Psychology and Children* (1969), 37, 42

Mays, J. B., *Education and the Urban Child* (1962), 52, 64
McDougall, W., *Introduction to Social Psychology* (1908), 9
Monroe, W. S., *Teacher-Learning, Theory and Teacher Education* (1952), 8, 17
Moreno, J. L., founder of sociometrics, 12

Morrison, A., and McIntyre, D., *Teachers and Teaching* (1969), 54, 64
Musgrove, F., and Taylor, P. H., *Society and the Teacher's Role* (1969), 55, 58, 64

Nunn, T. Percy, *Education: Its Data and First Principles* (1920), 9–10, 14

O'Connor, D. J., *Introduction to the Philosophy of Education* (1957), 94

Pavlov, I. P., 21
Peters, R. S., *The Concept of Education* (1966), *Ethics and Education* (1966), 14, 15, 94
Philosophy of education
  beginnings, 14
  case for philosophy, 80–2
  conceptual enquiry, 86–7
  further reading, 94
  'great educators' approach, 93
  grounds for belief, 87–8
  grouping of topics, 90–1
  the 'issues' approach, 93–4
  meanings of terms, 15
  main divisions, 91–2
  nature of subjects, 16
  its 'second order' character, 85
  topics of special interest, 88–9
  various approaches, 92–3
  what philosophy is, 82–4
Piaget, Jean, 10, 22–3, 31–2, 33, 35
Plowden Report, *Children and their Primary Schools* (1967), 49, 64
Psychology, educational
  beginnings, 7–8
  changes, 10
  child development, 31–2
  concepts, schema and transfer, 33–4
  ethology, 28–9
  examples, 20–5
  Freud and the emotions, 29–30
  imagination and creativity, 37–9
  in 1950s, 11
  intelligence and testing, 36–7
  language, 35–6
  nature of, 18–20, 25–6
  neurophysiology, 27–8
  perception, 29
  personality, 30–1
  Piaget, 34–5
  psychology and behaviour, 26–7
  social psychology, 39–40
  thinking and cognition, 32–3

Quick, R. H., *Essays on Educational Reformers* (1868), 7, 12

Reid, L. A., *Philosophy and Education* (1963), 94
Rosenthal, R. H., and Jacobson, L., *Pygmalion in the Classroom* (1968), 57, 64
Rowse, A. L., *The England of Elizabeth* (1950), 77
Rubinstein, D., *School attendance in London 1870–1904: a Social History* (1969), 77

Sadler, Michael, *Syllabus of Course on History of Education* (1911), 13
Scheffler, Israel, *The Language of Education* (1960), 15
Shipman, M., *Sociology of the School* (1968), 54, 64
Skinner, B. F., 22
Sociology of education
  aim, 45
  beginnings, 12
  concept of role, 46–8
  role
    of ancillary worker, 58–9
    of education in society, 59–60
    of parent, 57–8
    of pupil, 55–7
    of school, 48–52
    of teacher, 52–5
  sociology of education course, 60–3
Spearman, Charles, and selection tests, 10
Sprott, W. H. J., *Human Groups* (1958), 39, 43
Stones, E., *Introduction to Educational Psychology* (1966), 19, 36, 43

Sully, James, *Teacher's Handbook of Psychology* (1886), 7
Taylor, W., on aim of sociology of education, 45
Teacher training
  changes after 1902, 9, 65–6
  early stages, 5, 65
  Master of Method in, 8
  practical emphasis, 6
  1872 syllabus, 5–6
  1895 syllabus, 6–7
Theory and practice
  application to keeping discipline, 106
  learning to drive, 104–5
  nature of educational generalizations, 100–1
  necessity for judgment in application, 101–3
  normative function of theory, 109–10
  practical experience not enough, 107–8
  relationship between, 2, 6, 95–112
  starting with practice, 103–4
  theories as maps, 98
  unrealistic expectations of practitioners, 98–9
  utopian theorists, 96–7
  what freedom entails, 111–12
Thomson, Godfrey, and selection tests, 10
Thorndike, E. L., 21–2
Tropp, A., *The School Teachers* (1957), 53, 64

University departments of education, 13

Valentine, C. W., pioneer of child study, 10; *The Normal Child and Some of his Abnormalities* (1956), 25, 43

Waller, W., *The Sociology of Teaching* (1965), 47, 64
Walter, W. Grey, *The Living Brain* (1953), 28, 43
Watson, Foster, pioneer of history of education, 13
White, R. K., 24
Whitehead, A. N., *The Aims of Education* (1929), 14
Winch, W. H., pioneer of child study, 10
Wright, D. S., *Introducing Psychology* (1970), 27, 33, 35, 43

For Product Safety Concerns and Information please contact our EU representative GPSR@taylorandfrancis.com
Taylor & Francis Verlag GmbH, Kaufingerstraße 24, 80331 München, Germany

www.ingramcontent.com/pod-product-compliance
Lightning Source LLC
Chambersburg PA
CBHW061417300426
44114CB00015B/1972